1

MEGAWORDS

Multisyllabic Words for Reading, Spelling, and Vocabulary

POLLY BAYRD · KRISTIN JOHNSON

Educators Publishing Service

Cambridge and Toronto

Educators Publishing Service
800.225.5750
www.epsbooks.com

ISBN 0-8388-1826-9.

Design by Persis Barron Levy
5 6 7 8 CUR 09 08 07

CONTENTS

To the Student   iv

List 1: Compound Words   1

List 2: VC/CV Closed Syllables   9

List 3: VC/CV Closed and Silent-*e* Syllables   27

List 4: VC/CV Closed and *r*-Controlled Syllables   38

List 5: V/CV Syllabication Rule   53

List 6: VC/V Syllabication Rule   65

List 7: C*le* Syllabication Rule   78

List 8: V/V Syllabication Rule   89

Review: Lists 1-8   101

The Six Types of Syllables   102

The Five Syllabication Rules   102

Accuracy Checklist   103

Proficiency Graph   104

Examiner's Recording Form   107

TO THE STUDENT

Megawords 1: Multisyllabic Words for Reading, Spelling, and Vocabulary is the first in a series of books designed to help you read and spell words that contain two or more syllables. The words are organized into lists according to their phonetic structure. Worksheets following each list explain and help you practice the rules or patterns found in that particular group of words. Some exercises focus on reading the words; others focus on spelling or vocabulary.

Megawords is designed to meet your individual learning needs. You and your teacher can decide which lists you need to study (and which you already know) by interpreting your results on the Check Test. You may need to focus on reading *and* spelling. Or you may need to use **Megawords** only to improve spelling skills. You and your teacher can record your progress on the Accuracy Checklist at the back of your book.

We feel that it is important for you to be able to 1) sound out the words and 2) learn to read them proficiently and fluently. You and your teacher will set a reading rate goal. When you can read the words easily and automatically, you will be less likely to forget the words and you can concentrate on reading for meaning instead of sounding out words. You can keep track of your reading rate on the Proficiency Graph at the end of your book.

Megawords 1 focuses on six types of syllables and five rules for syllabication. **Megawords 1** assumes that you can already read and spell most one-syllable words, blend isolated sounds to form a syllable, and identify long and short vowels. It teaches you the different rules for dividing between syllables and helps you learn when to use each rule.

We hope that you will be interested in checking out your skills in reading and spelling multisyllabic words—in seeing what you know and what you need to learn. In addition, we hope that you will enjoy tackling new word groups and mastering them. We think that multisyllabic words, when presented clearly and in patterned groups, can be challenging and fun. We sincerely hope that you enjoy and experience success with **Megawords**.

Polly Bayrd
Kristin Johnson

* afternoon	* oatmeal	bluebird	moonlight
* airplane	* outfit	butterfly	newspaper
* anyone	* outside	cardboard	notebook
* anything	* popcorn	carload	outlaw
* anyway	* railroad	classroom	pancake
* baseball	* sidewalk	coconut	peanut
* become	* someone	cowhand	pineapple
* bedroom	* somewhere	daytime	playground
* belong	* strawberry	deckhand	playmate
* birthday	* sunshine	driveway	pocketbook
* breakfast	* today	drugstore	raincoat
* everyone	* tonight	fishhook	sailboat
* everything	* understood	friendship	snowball
* everywhere	* without	gentleman	snowflake
* football	* yourself	grapefruit	snowshoe
* footstep	airport	graveyard	somebody
* forget	anywhere	handball	something
* forgive	background	haystack	sometimes
* forgot	backpack	headache	streetcar
* grandfather	barefoot	herself	washtub
* grandmother	battleship	himself	wastebasket
* maybe	bedspread	homesick	workshop
* myself	below	horseback	
* necktie	beside	lookout	

*Practical spelling words. The teacher and student should decide together how many of these words the student will be responsible for spelling.

➤ **A compound word** is made of two small words that combine to make a new word. *Class/room* and *snow/shoe* are examples. Pronounce and combine the small words to read the compound word. Then circle the small words as shown.

news	paper	(news)(paper)•	snow	shoe	snowshoe•
some	body	somebody	out	law	outlaw•
any	one	anyone•	sun	shine	sunshine•
class	room	classroom•	card	board	cardboard•
grave	yard	graveyard•	drive	way	driveway•
air	plane	airplane•	rain	coat	raincoat•
butter	fly	butterfly•	drug	store	drugstore•

➤ Match the small words to make a compound word. Then say the compound word to yourself as you write it on the line.

may	pack	_____ •	bed	self	_____ •
back	body	_____ •	cow	road	_____ •
some	ground	_____ •	him	day	_____ •
play	be	*maybe* •	rail	long	_____ •
neck	book	_____ •	birth	hand	_____ •
note	tie	_____ •	be	room	_____ •

➤ Find and circle the twenty-five words above that have a • after them. The words can be found in a straight line across or up and down.

```
N C L A S S R O O M R A I N C O A T B E L O N G
O A N Y O N E S E A A N T C E N E W S P A P E R
T B D R I V E W A Y I P L A Y G R O U N D M C A
E S N O W S H O E B L E N C O B A C K P A C K V
B B I R T H D A Y E R R R B U T T E R F L Y T E
O U T L A W E C T T O H C A R D B O A R D E I Y
O S U N S H I N E A A X S H O A I R P L A N E A
K H I M S E L F B E D R O O M W N A C G P T K R
D R U G S T O R E S O M E B O D Y C O W H A N D
```

➡ *Any, some,* and *every* are often found at the beginning of compound words. Write them in the blanks; then copy the whole word.

any	**Copy**	**some**	**Copy**
_____where	_____	_____where	_____
_____way	_____	_____body	_____
_____one	_____	_____one	_____
_____thing	_____	_____thing	_____
_____body	_____		

every	**Copy**	**every**	**Copy**
_____where	_____	_____one	_____
_____body	_____	_____thing	_____

➡ *Self* and *where* are often found at the end of compound words. Write them in the blanks; then copy the whole word.

self	**Copy**	**where**	**Copy**
your_____	_____	any_____	_____
it_____	_____	every_____	_____
my_____	_____	some_____	_____
her_____	_____	no_____	_____

➡ *Be* and *out* can be found at the beginning or the end of compound words. Write them in the blanks; then copy the whole world.

be	**Copy**	**out**	**Copy**
_____side	_____	look_____	_____
_____low	_____	_____law	_____
_____come	_____	with_____	_____
may_____	_____	_____side	_____
_____long	_____		

➡ Your teacher will dictate ten compound words. Locate the word parts and then write the compound word in the space provided.

side	plane	1. __lookout__
air	mother	2. _____
~~look~~	load	3. _____
pop	corn	4. _____
any	walk	5. _____
car	~~out~~	6. _____
grand	one	7. _____
hand	board	8. _____
card	store	9. _____
drug	ball	10. _____

➡ Your teacher will dictate some compound words. Spell the first word and then write the compound word on the lines provided.

11. _____road   _____

12. _____ball   _____

13. _____be   _____

14. _____where   _____

15. _____hook   _____

➡ Spell the second word and then write the compound word on the lines provided.

16. snow _____   _____

17. back _____   _____

18. hay _____   _____

19. with _____   _____

20. bed _____   _____

➡ Divide these compound words by drawing a line between the small words. Write the two smaller words on the lines provided. Say them aloud as you spell.

horse/back _____horse_____   _____back_____

pancake _____   _____

playmate _____   _____

sailboat _____   _____

Sunday _____   _____

outside _____   _____

sometimes _____   _____

moonlight _____   _____

driveway _____   _____

snowball _____   _____

peanut _____   _____

playground _____   _____

tonight _____   _____

yourself _____   _____

forgive _____   _____

washtub _____   _____

lookout _____   _____

bluebird _____   _____

snowflake _____   _____

Proofing Practice

➡ Two common List 1 words are misspelled in each of the sentences below. Correct them as shown.

1. A ~~burthday~~ *birthday* is no fun withowt cake and ice cream.

2. Will someone please order oatmeel for the football player's breckfast?

3. Tonite I heard footsteps on the driveway outsid my grandmother's bedroom.

➡ Your teacher will dictate ten compound words. Write the smaller words on the first two lines and then combine them on the third line to make the compound word. Say the words aloud as you spell them.

Sample ___air___ ___port___ ___airport___

1. _____ _____ _____
2. _____ _____ _____
3. _____ _____ _____
4. _____ _____ _____
5. _____ _____ _____
6. _____ _____ _____
7. _____ _____ _____
8. _____ _____ _____
9. _____ _____ _____
10. _____ _____ _____

Review

A _____ word is made of two small words that combine to make a new word (*class/room, snow/shoe*).

➡ Fill in the puzzle with the words from above.

Across
2. morning meal
4. opposite of inside
5. a thing that is not definite
6. room where you sleep
7. the mark your footprint leaves
8. this evening
9. perhaps

Down
1. opposite of remembered
2. to be a part of
3. anybody

➡ Some compound words can be taken apart to make a definition.

1. A bedspread can be ___spread___ on a ___bed___ .

2. A sidewalk is a place to _____ on the _____ of the road.

3. A raincoat is a _____ to use in the _____ .

4. A sailboat is a _____ with a _____ .

5. A necktie is something you can _____ around your _____ .

6. A wastebasket is a _____ for _____ .

7. A fishhook is a _____ for catching _____ .

8. Popcorn is _____ that you _____ .

9. A haystack is a _____ of _____ .

10. A notebook is a _____ to use for writing a _____ .

11. A bluebird is a _____ that is _____ .

12. A washtub is a _____ for the _____ .

➡ Write the correct compound words in the blanks.

forgot	outlaw	snowshoes	backpack	belong
maybe	pineapples	oatmeal	grapefruit	forgive
himself	outside	birthday	coconuts	

1. _____, _____, and _____ are
   three fruits that grow in warm places.

2. _____ is a hot cereal made from oats.

3. The _____ gave _____ up to the police.

4. Do not take things that don't _____ to you.

5. _____ we can go _____ when it stops raining.

6. Joanne took her _____ and _____ when she went
   camping in the snow.

7. I could not _____ myself if I _____ your
   _____ .

➤ Read the following sentences and circle all the List 1 words that you can find.

1. Luisa and her grandmother bought her grandfather a necktie for his birthday.

2. The deckhand on the battleship saw a sailboat in the moonlight.

3. The cowhand rode horseback past the graveyard.

4. Kim and her playmate like to skate on the sidewalk near the playground.

5. The gentlemen ate oatmeal for breakfast.

6. Everyone at the football game ate popcorn.

7. Be on the lookout for a carload of boys and girls carrying showshoes.

8. The bedspread hung outside to dry in the sunshine.

9. Sometimes Derek forgets to do his chores in the afternoon.

10. The airport is six miles from the railroad track.

11. Someone will understand what Tom wrote in his notebook.

➤ Take out a piece of blank paper. Your teacher will dictate three of the sentences above for you to write.

➤ Now select ten words from List 1 and create a short story or a descriptive paragraph that uses those words. Be creative and avoid repetition!

Reading Accuracy: Demonstrate your accuracy in reading and spelling List 1 words. Your teacher will select ten words to read and ten practical spelling words for you to spell. Record your scores on the Accuracy Checklist. Work toward 90–100 percent accuracy.

Reading Proficiency: Now build up your reading fluency with List 1 words. Decide on your rate goal with your teacher. Record your progress on the Proficiency Graph.

My goal for reading List 1 is _____ words per minute with two or fewer errors.

LIST 2: VC/CV CLOSED SYLLABLES

/ă/		/ă/	/ĕ/	/ĭ/	/ŏ/	/ŭ/
* absent	candid		* dentist	* children	* blossom	* button
* address	canyon		* lesson	* kitten	* bonnet	* hundred
* attic	catnip		* selfish	* picnic	* bottom	* husband
* basket	channel		* tennis	* pilgrim	* common	* public
* blanket	Dallas		Bettina	* ribbon	* congress	* pumpkin
* gallon	flannel		dental	* signal	* contest	* subject
* happen	frantic		enchant	chipmunk	* cotton	* subtract
* napkin	gallop		hectic	infant	* object	* sudden
* rabbit	magnet		mental	infect	* problem	* until
* sandwich	mammal		pretzel	insect	coffin	custom
* tablet	mantis		seldom	insult	collect	humbug
actress	mascot		splendid	kidnap	connect	muffin
annex	random		tendon	mitten	conquest	musket
atlas	sandal		velvet	Phillip	consent	nutmeg
bandit	talcum			pistol	contact	publish
cactus	traffic			quintet	convict	puppet
campus				tinsel	fossil	trumpet
				wisdom	goblet	tunnel
					goblin	
					gossip	
					optic	
					ostrich	
					progress	
					tonsil	

Three-Syllable Words

* Atlantic
* establish
* fantastic
badminton
Wisconsin

*Practical spelling words. The teacher and student should decide together how many of these words the student will be responsible for spelling.

9

TYPES OF SYLLABLES The Closed Syllable (VC)

A **syllable** is a group of letters that has a single vowel sound. Some syllables are **closed.**★ There are three things to remember about the **closed syllable (VC):**

1. It has only one vowel.

2. The vowel has a short sound.

3. It ends in a consonant.

➤ Circle only those syllables below that are closed syllables. Then copy them under the headings below according to their vowel sound. Pronounce the syllables, giving the vowel its short sound.

gos	pret	trum	cade	lish
fle	sud	op	flan	prob
tal	cu	hus	sel	tain
vict	tist	caul	ject	ap
blos	lete	chil	tact	ple

/ă/ as in *apple*	/ĭ/ as in *igloo*	/ŏ/ as in *octopus*
_____	_____	_____
_____	_____	_____
_____	_____	_____
_____	_____	_____

/ŭ/ as in *umbrella*	/ĕ/ as in *Ed*
_____	_____
_____	_____
_____	_____

★A summary of the six types of syllables is on page 102.

Review

If a syllable is a **closed syllable,** you know the vowel sound must be _____. You can tell if a syllable is closed because it will have only _____ vowel and it will always end in a _____.

➤ Write *closed* if the syllable is closed and mark the vowel short. If the syllable is not closed, explain why.

pŭs   *closed*
       no consonant at end,
loo   *2 vowels*

cle   _____

vel   _____

mu   _____

os   _____

tume   _____

min   _____

crea   _____

prob   _____

li   _____

com   _____

lope   _____

trich _____

nee   _____

plode _____

nex   _____

gra   _____

sil   _____

ple   _____

EXCEPTION

When *qu* is found in a word, the *u* does not have a vowel sound and will always be followed by a vowel. Therefore, the following syllables are closed. Pronounce them, giving the vowel its short sound.

quin   quest   quiv   ques

➡ Syllables in long words often end in the consonant blend *ct*. Many students have trouble spelling this because it is hard to hear. Add *ct* to the end of each syllable below and then write the whole syllable, pronouncing it aloud as you spell.

fe _____   _____   vi _____   _____

se _____   _____   ta _____   _____

je _____   _____   le _____   _____

If you hear a short-vowel sound in a syllable, what kind of syllable will it be? _____

How many vowels will it have? _____ What kind of letter will the last letter be? _____

➡ Your teacher will dictate twelve closed syllables. Repeat the syllables aloud while spelling them.

1. _____   7. _____

2. _____   8. _____

3. _____   9. _____

4. _____   10. _____

5. _____   11. _____

6. _____   12. _____

➡ Circle the *-ct* syllable in these words.

infect   dejected   evict   detractor

reject   insect   tactical   elect

select   injected   subtract   convict

subject   subtracting   convicted   insecticide

➡ Many words are made by putting two closed syllables together. The vowel sounds in these syllables will be
_____. Mark the vowels short (˘); then pronounce the syllables and combine them to read
the whole word. Circle the syllables as shown.

cŏn	tăct	(con)(tact)
nut	meg	nutmeg
mas	cot	mascot
pub	lish	publish
con	vict	convict
hec	tic	hectic
at	tic	attic
un	til	until

ad	dress	address
con	test	contest
in	sect	insect
sel	fish	selfish
quin	tet	quintet
cac	tus	cactus
tal	cum	talcum

➡ Fill in the blanks with one of the words from above.

1. kind of desert plant _____

2. chance for someone to win _____

3. thinking only of oneself _____

4. bug _____

5. type of powder _____

6. a group of five _____

7. a spice _____

8. person in prison _____

9. space just below the roof _____

10. tells where to send mail _____

★ Often when two closed syllables are combined to make a two-syllable word, the vowel in the second syllable is not short. Instead it will have a short-*i* or the *schwa* sound, which sounds like a short *u* /ŭ/. The schwa sound is the same for all vowels and is marked with the symbol /ə/. The schwa sound is found only in the unaccented syllable, which is usually the second syllable of a two-syllable word.

➡ Mark the first vowel short / ˘ /. Pronounce and combine the syllables to read the whole word. Then circle the syllables as shown.

băn	dit	(ban)(dit)
gob	lin	goblin
pret	zel	pretzel
tin	sel	tinsel
vel	vet	velvet
sub	ject	subject
ton	sil	tonsil

kit	ten	kitten
hus	band	husband
hap	pen	happen
san	dal	sandal
bas	ket	basket
sel	dom	seldom
gal	lon	gallon

➡ Fill in the blanks with one of the words from above.

1. male spouse _____

2. not often _____

3. an ugly-looking elf _____

4. robber _____

5. used to trim Christmas trees _____

6. type of summer shoe _____

7. thick, soft cloth _____

8. something to snack on _____

➡ Match the syllables to make a real word. Then say it as you write it.

mag	vict		prog	ress		hun	wich
	tom			nel			dred
	net			dom			pen

___*magnet*___   _____   _____

sel	sip		ton	sil		fran	tic
	meg			let			vet
	fish			nap			nel

_____   _____   _____

➡ Match the syllables to make real words.

den	zel	_____	trum	dom	_____
hus	tist	_____	sel	nel	_____
pret	band	_____	tun	pet	_____

con	tus	_____	prob	nel	_____
cac	den	_____	flan	tress	_____
sud	test	_____	ac	lem	_____

➡ Unscramble these three-syllable words.

tas	tic	fan	_____
lish	es	tab	_____
bad	ton	min	_____
lan	At	tic	_____
sin	con	Wis	_____

➡ Your teacher will dictate twenty words. Repeat the word, isolate the missing syllable, and spell the syllable. Then write the whole word, saying it aloud as you spell it.

1. _____ cum   _____

2. _____ ket   _____

3. _____ bon   _____

4. _____ did   _____

5. _____ tract   _____

6. _____ tus   _____

7. _____ pet   _____

8. _____ trich   _____

9. _____ dom   _____

10. _____ nap   _____

11. _____ tist   _____

12. _____ lem   _____

13. kid _____   _____

14. sel _____   _____

15. in _____   _____

16. con _____   _____

17. cac _____   _____

18. nut _____   _____

19. con _____   _____

20. es tab _____   _____

Review

Cross out the incorrect letter or word in each parentheses.

A closed syllable has (one, two) vowel(s). The vowel has a (long, short) sound. The syllable ends in a (vowel, consonant).

Review

The second syllable of a two-syllable word often has the short-*i* sound or the schwa sound /ə/. The schwa sound can be difficult to spell because all of the vowels can make the sound and you have to remember which vowel to use.

➤ *et* is a common spelling for the /ət/ or /ĭt/ sound at the end of words. Fill in the blank with *et*, copy the whole word, and then arrange the words in alphabetical order.

	Copy	**ABC Order**
gob l _____	_____	_____
bas k _____	_____	_____
pup p _____	_____	_____
blan k _____	_____	_____
vel v _____	_____	_____
mag n _____	_____	_____
trum p _____	_____	_____
tab l _____	_____	_____
bon n _____	_____	_____

➤ Use the words above to match the definitions below.

1. a horn _____

2. a soft fabric _____

3. a toy _____

4. a bed cover _____

5. a fancy glass with a stem _____

6. a pad of paper _____

7. something that attracts metal _____

8. a straw container _____

9. a type of hat _____

➤ *ic* is a common spelling for the /ĭk/ sound at the end of two- and three-syllable words. Fill in the missing syllable *tic* and match the words to the definitions.

fran _____   1. having to do with the eye_____

At lan _____   2. super!_____

op _____   3. wild with pain or fear_____

hec _____   4. large ocean_____

at _____   5. confusing; filled with excitement_____

fan tas _____   6. space just below the roof_____

➤ *om* is a common way to spell the /əm/ sound at the end of words. Fill in the blank with *om* and match the words to the definitions.

ran d_____   7. flower _____

cus t_____   8. by chance _____

sel d_____   9. habit _____

blos s_____   10. lowest part _____

bot t_____   11. not often _____

problem   probl__ __   __ro__l__m   p__ __b__ __m

Review

How do you spell these common endings?

/ət/   =   _____   as in bask _____

/ĭk/   =   _____   as in att _____

/əm/   =   _____   as in bott _____

RULE

The **VC/CV Syllabication Rule** is the first of five rules★ that will help you sound out long words. The VC/CV Rule says that when two or more consonants (C) stand between two vowels (V), you divide between the consonants. The first vowel will usually be short because it will be in a closed syllable.

In List 2 words, the second syllable is also closed and the second vowel will either be short / ˘ / or schwa /ə/.

➡ Follow these directions:

1. Outline the vowels in red.
2. Place a dot between the consonants.
3. Draw an arc underneath the syllables.
4. Mark the first vowel short.
5. Read the words to your teacher or another student.
6. Then complete the puzzle.

Example: selfish

discuss   (17 Across)

frantic   (7 Down)

pretzel   (1 Down)

until   (4 Down)

talcum   (15 Across)

tinsel   (11 Down)

tonsil   (14 Across)

tendon   (9 Down)

optic   (2 Down)

dental   (6 Across)

contact   (13 Across)

progress   (1 Across)

magnet   (8 Across)

mantis   (3 Down)

mascot   (10 Down)

random   (5 Down)

quintet   (16 Across)

annex   (12 Across)

★A summary of the five syllabication rules is on page 102.

The **VC/CV Syllabication Rule** says that if two or more consonants stand between two vowels, divide between the _____. The first vowel will usually have a _____ sound because it will be in a _____ syllable.

➡ If more than two consonants stand between two vowels, divide between the consonants, keeping consonant blends (*tr, dr, nd,* etc.) and digraphs (*th, ch, sh, wh*) together. Circle the blends and digraphs. Divide these words into syllables and pronounce them.

	First Syllable	**Second Syllable**
Example: congress	con	gress
hundred	_____	_____
pumpkin	_____	_____
ostrich	_____	_____
pilgrim	_____	_____
actress	_____	_____
address	_____	_____
enchant	_____	_____
children	_____	_____
sandwich	_____	_____

➡ Use the VC/CV Rule to divide these three-syllable words.

	First Syllable	**Second Syllable**	**Third Syllable**
establish	_____	_____	_____
badminton	_____	_____	_____
fantastic	_____	_____	_____
Wisconsin	_____	_____	_____
Atlantic	_____	_____	_____

★ When you hear the /ən/ sound at the end of two-syllable words, you will use one of the following spellings:

Choice #1	on	as in	ribbon
Choice #2	en	as in	kitten
Choice #3	in	as in	napkin

➡ Circle the last two letters in each of the following words. Then write the words under the correct heading.

*napkin   *happen   *cotton   coffin   *pumpkin   *kitten

*sudden   *children   *gallon   *common   tendon   *button

muffin   *lesson   Wisconsin   mitten   *ribbon   badminton

on Words	*en* Words	*in* Words
_____	_____	_____
_____	_____	_____
_____	_____	_____
_____	_____	_____
_____	_____	_____
_____		
_____		
_____		

The words that are starred are common words. Be sure that you learn how spell these words.

➡ Fill in the blanks with the starred words.

Dad was driving the _____ to their tennis _____ when all of a

_____ the car ran out of gas. They all walked to get a _____ of gas. On

the way, Erika lost her hair _____, a _____ fell off Evan's

_____ shirt, and Eric found a lost _____. What would _____

next?

★ Usually, a short vowel in the first syllable of a multisyllabic word must be followed by two consonants. If you hear one consonant sound between two vowels, you must remember to double the middle consonant.

➤ Can you figure out the following words? Say the syllables aloud as you spell the words.

child's toy	pu __ __ et	_____
used to tie something	ri __ __ on	* _____
game two people play	te __ __ is	* _____
baby cat	ki __ __ en	* _____
lowest part	bo __ __ om	* _____
humans, cats, dogs, horses	ma __ __ als	_____
faster than a trot	ga __ __ op	_____
talk about other people	go __ __ ip	_____
four quarts	ga __ __ on	* _____
used to bury people	co __ __ in	_____
an underground passage	tu __ __ el	_____
something added on	a __ __ ex	_____
type of cloth	co __ __ on	* _____
type of cloth	fla __ __ el	_____
usual	co __ __ on	* _____
small, round cake or bread	mu __ __ in	_____
something to be learned	le __ __ on	* _____
to fasten	bu __ __ on	* _____
just below the roof	a __ __ ic	_____

➤ Have another student test you on spelling the starred words. They are practical spelling words.

My score: _____ words correct.

➡ Directions:

    1. Your teacher will dictate a two- or three-syllable word.
    2. Repeat the word.
    3. Isolate and pronounce the first syllable, saying the sounds as you spell.
    4. Isolate and pronounce the second and third syllables, saying the sounds as you spell.
    5. Combine the syllables and write the whole word, saying the sounds as you spell.

1. | | | _____

2. | | | _____

3. | | | _____

4. | | | _____

5. | | | _____

6. | | | _____

7. | | | _____

8. | | | _____

9. | | | | _____

10. | | | | _____

➡ Fill in the blanks with words from above.

1. All of a _____ Allen dropped the picnic _____.

2. The new _____ plans to _____ herself in this office.

3. Miguel was so _____ that he had a _____ making friends.

➤ Here are more words from List 2 that you are likely to use in writing. Be sure that you learn how to spell these words. Fill in the blanks with words that make sense in the sentences.

absent	napkins	dentist	tennis	sandwich
until	selfish	rabbit	hundred	subject
address	contest	husband	problem	insect

1. Michelle's best _____ is math. She got one _____ percent on the test.

2. I have to go to the _____ to get a tooth filled.

3. Let's play _____ _____ 4:00 p.m.

4. Alex was _____ from school on the day we had the spelling _____.

5. Please fix me a ham _____ for lunch.

6. If you give Emma your _____, she can write you a letter.

7. An _____ bit me.

8. Nick is very _____. His _____ is that he only cares about himself.

9. A _____ was eating the flowers in our backyard. My _____ set out a trap to catch it.

10. Be sure to put _____ on the table.

➤ Now have another student test you on spelling these common words.

My score: _____ words correct.

Proofing Practice

➤ Two common List 2 words are misspelled in each of the sentences below. Correct them as shown.

                                              absent

1. How did it happen that Nick was ~~abbsent~~ from his first tennus class?

2. Keeping insects away from your sandwitch at a picnick is a common problem.

3. Pilgrims crossed the Atlantick Ocean to esstablish new homes.

➡ Each of the following sentences can be improved by using a word from the bottom of the page in place of the words that are underlined. Write the correct word to the right of each sentence. Use your dictionary to help you.

1. The bear is the <u>good luck animal</u> for the Chicago football team.

   _____

2. My sister wrote a book that will be <u>printed</u> next year.

   _____

3. I gave Ingrid a set of <u>drinking glasses</u> for her wedding.

   _____

4. Humans, horses, dogs, lions, and whales are all <u>animals that feed milk to their young.</u>

   _____

5. Jennifer was not listening and gave a <u>chance</u> anwer to the teacher's question.

   _____

6. The United States <u>added</u> Alaska and Hawaii as new states.

   _____

7. Olivia hurt a <u>piece of tissue that joins muscle to bone</u> when she was playing football.

   _____

8. Richard was very <u>frank</u> about his reasons for wanting to change jobs.

   _____

9. We want this <u>insect</u> in our flower bed because it eats other insects.

   _____

10. The <u>group of five players</u> had a trumpet, a sax, a bass, a keyboard, and a set of drums.

    _____

11. We call the old man a <u>cheater</u> because he pretends to be something other than what he is.

    _____

12. The <u>eye</u> nerve connects the eye to the brain.

    _____

mammals	tendon	annexed	candid	goblets	humbug
quintet	mantis	optic	published	random	mascot

➡ Read the following sentences and circle all the List 2 words that you can find.

1. Nicole took a basket of food and a blanket to the picnic.

2. Cindy wrote notes on her tablet about her best subject.

3. The tennis team had a chipmunk as its mascot.

4. The children had a splendid time playing with the kitten.

5. Please get me a gallon of milk, a bag of pretzels, and some nutmeg at the store.

6. Donna played her trumpet at the campus pub.

7. It is common to have problems with your wisdom teeth.

8. What will happen if Phillip's tonsils get infected?

9. You will get a blue ribbon if you win the contest.

10. The actress ate a pumpkin muffin and a sandwich.

11. Contact me if you and your husband want to join us for a game of badminton.

➡ Take out a piece of blank paper. Your teacher will dictate three of the sentences above for you to write.

➡ Now select ten words from List 2 and create a short story or a descriptive paragraph that uses those words. Be creative and avoid repetition!

Reading Accuracy: Demonstrate your accuracy in reading and spelling List 2 words. Your teacher will select ten words to read and ten practical spelling words for you to spell. Record your scores on the Accuracy Checklist. Work toward 90–100 percent accuracy.

Reading Proficiency: Now build up your reading fluency with List 2 words. Decide on your rate goal with your teacher. Record your progress on the Proficiency Graph.

My goal for reading List 2 is _____ words per minute with two or fewer errors.

/ā/	/ē/	/ī/	/ō/	/ū/ and /o͞o/
* escape	* compete	* collide	backbone	* compute
* estate	* complete	* combine	backstroke	* conclude
* mistake	* concrete	* describe	compote	* confuse
* pancake	athlete	* entire	enclose	* costume
cascade	extreme	* incline	explode	* dispute
compare	stampede	* inquire	explore	* excuse
dictate		* inside	expose	* include
inflate		* invite	ignore	accuse
inhale		* retire	oppose	commune
insane		* sunshine	suppose	consume
invade		* umpire	tadpole	immune
landscape		admire	trombone	intrude
membrane		advice		pollute
octane		advise		
stagnate		baptize		
translate		confide		
welfare		connive		
		contrive		
		empire		
		hemline		
		ignite		
		pastime		
		reptile		
		subscribe		
		sunrise		
		textile		

Three-Syllable Words

compensate	indispose
confiscate	infantile
contemplate	infiltrate
illustrate	

*Practical spelling words. The teacher and student should decide together how many of these words the student will be responsible for spelling.

TYPES OF SYLLABLES | The Silent-*e* Syllable (VC*e*)

A **silent-*e* syllable (VC*e*)** has one vowel followed by a consonant followed by an *e*. The *e* is silent and makes the preceding vowel long (āce, hīde, dōme).

Review

A **closed syllable (VC)** has only one vowel, ends in a consonant, and has a short-vowel sound (trŏm, ĕm, jĕct).

➡ The following syllables are either *silent-e* or *closed*. Write them in the correct columns.

pire	pas	rise	con	trive
cuse	tane	vade	pede	flate
trom	stag	wel	in	sume
en	ig	mem	treme	rep

Silent-*e* Syllables		**Closed Syllables**	
1. _____	6. _____	1. _____	6. _____
2. _____	7. _____	2. _____	7. _____
3. _____	8. _____	3. _____	8. _____
4. _____	9. _____	4. _____	9. _____
5. _____	10. _____	5. _____	10. _____

➡ Your teacher will dictate ten syllables. Repeat each syllable and write it under the correct column.

Silent-*e* Syllables	**Closed Syllables**
_____	_____
_____	_____
_____	_____
_____	_____
_____	_____

➡ Circle the silent-*e* syllables in the words below.

empire   invade   contrive   extreme   consume

The **VC/CV Syllabication Rule:** When two or more consonants stand between two vowels, divide between the consonants keeping blends and digraphs together. This makes the first syllable closed and the vowel sound short.

➡ Pronounce and combine the syllables to read the whole word.

in	vade	in/vade
en	close	enclose
em	pire	empire
oc	tane	octane
col	lide	collide
ex	treme	extreme

dic	tate	dictate
cas	cade	cascade
rep	tile	reptile
con	crete	concrete
cos	stume	costume
um	pire	umpire

➡ Now look the words over again. Mark between the syllables with a slash. Underline the closed syllables, and circle the silent-*e* syllables as shown above.

➡ Work with three-syllable words. Pronounce and combine the syllables to read the whole word.

com	pen	sate	com/pen/sate
il	lus	trate	illustrate
con	tem	plate	contemplate
in	fan	tile	infantile
in	dis	pose	indispose
con	fis	cate	confiscate

➡ Now look the words over again. Mark between the syllables with a slash. Underline the closed syllables and circle the silent-*e* syllables as shown above.

Where are the closed syllables? _____

Where are the silent-*e* syllables? _____

➡ Match the syllables to make a real word. Then say it as you write it.

im	lete	_athlete_	trom	vade	_____
es	mune	_____	con	pole	_____
ath	pede	_____	in	bone	_____
stam	cape	_____	tad	crete	_____

con	tume	_____	ig	tile	_____
cos	take	_____	com	nite	_____
mis	plode	_____	bap	mune	_____
ex	fide	_____	rep	tize	_____

➡ Reorder the syllables to make a recognizable three-syllable word.

sate	com	pen	_____
con	cate	fis	_____
fan	in	tile	_____
trate	lus	il	_____
in	trate	fil	_____

➡ Your teacher will dictate ten words. Listen carefully and fill in the missing syllable, saying it aloud as you spell. Then write the whole word.

1. _____ pire   _____

2. _____ crete   _____

3. _____ nore   _____

4. _____ pole   _____

5. _____ plore   _____

6. in _____   _____

7. dic _____   _____

8. in _____   _____

9. oc _____   _____

10. stag _____   _____

Review the Rules

A _____ syllable has only one vowel, ends in a consonant, and has a short-vowel sound.

A _____ syllable has one long vowel followed by one consonant followed by an *e*.

The *e* is silent and makes the preceding vowel long.

The VC/CV Syllabication Rule that when two or more _____ stand between

two _____, you divide between the _____, keeping

blends and digraphs together.

Closed Syllable

_____ vowel, ends in a

_____; has a

_____-vowel sound.

Silent-*e* Syllable

_____ vowel followed by

_____ consonant followed

by an _____; has a

_____-vowel sound.

➡ Directions:

1. Outline the vowels in red.
2. Place a dot between the consonants. (Remember that consonant blends or digraphs stay together.)
3. Draw an arc underneath the syllables.
4. Mark the vowels with the correct long (-) or short (˘) sign.
5. Read the words to your teacher or another student.

băp·tīze   empire   trombone   dictate   explore   athlete

expose   sunshine   invite   cascade   reptile   illustrate

stagnate   stampede   intrude   costume   concrete   infantile

➡ In six of these words, a consonant blend or digraph was kept together. Write them down by syllables, circling the blend or digraph. The first one is done for you.

sun_____   (sh)ine_____   _____   _____

_____   _____   _____   _____

_____   _____   _____   _____

➡ Find and circle all of the words above in the puzzle below. The words can be found in a straight line across or up or down.

```
I N T R U D E E X P L O R E P T I L E T E S
M O R E P T I S T A M P E D E I N V I T X U
V B O C O S T U M E E A X R M E V I C O R N
I A M P I R E N O M E M P I R E I M P I R S
T P B T R A N S L A T E O L O A T H L E T E
R T O M B O N H I N C A S C A D E O O X R S
A I N F A N T I L E N E E O D U C T R I A O
N Z E S T A G N A T E I L L U S T R A T E M
S E C O N C R E T E D I C T A T E X M I N E
```

➡ Divide between the consonants (VC/CV). Circle the consonant blends or digraphs that stay together. Then pronounce the word as you write it by syllables on the lines provided.

	First Syllable	**Second Syllable**
escape	_es_	_cape_
inquire		
complete		
dispute		
translate		
admire		
extreme		
ignore		

➡ In these words, the first syllable is _____ and the vowel has a _____ sound.

The last syllable is _____ and the vowel has a _____ sound.

➡ These words follow the VC/CV pattern. There is only one middle consonant sound; remember to double that consonant. Then pronounce the word as you write it by syllables.

connive	co_n_ _n_ive	_con_	_nive_
collide	co__ __ide		
oppose	o__ __ose		
suppose	su__ __ose		
commune	co__ __une		
accuse	a__ __use		
pollute	po__ __ute		
immune	i__ __une		

→ Directions:

     1. Your teacher will dictate ten two-syllable words.
     2. Repeat the word.
     3. Isolate and pronounce the first syllable, saying the sounds as you spell.
     4. Isolate and pronounce the second syllable, saying the sounds as you spell.
     5. Combine the syllables and write the whole word, saying the sounds as you spell.

1. ☐ ☐ _____

2. ☐ ☐ _____

3. ☐ ☐ _____

4. ☐ ☐ _____

5. ☐ ☐ _____

6. ☐ ☐ _____

7. ☐ ☐ _____

8. ☐ ☐ _____

9. ☐ ☐ _____

10. ☐ ☐ _____

Proofing Practice

→ Two common List 3 words are misspelled in each of the sentences below. Correct them as shown.

                                              collide
1. Good athletes try not to dispute when they ~~colide~~ by misteak.

2. Do you suppose the umpire will retir after he compleats his contract?

3. We'll invite the intire cast to a costoom party after the show.

➡ Match each word to its definition.

connive	a thin, soft layer of plant or animal tissue
stagnate	to become stale and inactive
confiscate	to work together secretly
membrane	to take away

➡ Fill in the blanks with the correct words from the list below.

1. The mucous _____ is in your nose.

2. The water in the pond will _____ unless the dam is opened.

3. The _____ grew into a frog.

4. Our class spent all our time at the zoo in the _____ house watching the snakes.

5. The _____ called the ball a foul.

6. The horses _____d when they heard the gunshot.

7. She _____d about a room in the hotel.

8. The two teams _____d each other on the playing field.

9. The customs officer will _____ the fruit from the islands.

10. The bandits will _____ to rob the bank.

11. The Roman _____ ruled over many countries.

12. Patrick is not _____d to try out for the football team. He loves basketball.

umpire	reptile	stampede	tadpole
incline	oppose	empire	membrane
stagnate	inquire	confiscate	connive

➡ Complete the puzzle with the following words.

reptile	extreme	inflate	accuse	empire
concrete	dispute	infantile	trombone	dictate
intrude	textile	escape	collide	

Across

3. a large brass musical instrument

4. to blow up with air

5. like a baby

8. to say or read aloud; to make

11. argue, debate

12. a cold-blooded animal that creeps or crawls

13. a mixture of cement, sand, and water

14. to run away

Down

1. to rush against, to bump into

2. to force oneself on others without being asked or wanted

6. to charge with having done something wrong

7. a country with lots of power others obey

9. woven fabric

10. very great; very strong; at the very end

➡ Read the following sentences and circle all the List 3 words that you can find.

1. It is hard not to collide with other swimmers when doing the backstroke.

2. The athlete hurt his backbone by jogging on concrete.

3. I advise you to compare prices before you subscribe to this newspaper.

4. Arnell admired the sunrise in the landscape.

5. Don't confuse me anymore with your advice.

6. Watching the sunrise is one of my favorite pastimes.

7. If we do not enclose the horses in a pen, they may stampede.

8. Justin made a mistake when he computed that problem.

9. It would be insane to to eat 100 pancakes.

10. The fans will dispute the umpire's call.

➡ Take out a piece of blank paper. Your teacher will dictate three of the sentences above for you to write.

➡ Now select ten words from List 3 and create a short story or a descriptive paragraph that uses those words. Be creative and avoid repetition!

Reading Accuracy: Demonstrate your accuracy in reading and spelling List 3 words. Your teacher will select ten words to read and ten practical spelling words for you to spell. Record your scores on the Accuracy Checklist. Work toward 90–100 percent accuracy.

Reading Proficiency: Now build up your reading fluency with List 3 words. Decide on your rate goal with your teacher. Record your progress on the Proficiency Graph.

My goal for reading List 3 is _____ words per minute with two or fewer errors.

LIST 4: VC/CV CLOSED AND r-CONTROLLED SYLLABLES

-er- = /er/	-er- = /er/	-er- = /er/	-ar- = /ar/	-or- = /or/	-ur- = /er/ -ir- = /er/
* anger	* servant	Robert	* artist	* correct	* circle
* better	* silver	serpent	* barber	* forest	* thirsty
* bitter	* slipper	sherbet	* carbon	* organ	* turkey
* butter	* suffer	slender	* farmer	absorb	absurd
* chapter	* summer	temper	* garden	afford	burden
* copper	* supper	timber	* garment	border	circus
* differ	* tender	verdict	* market	corner	confirm
* dinner	* thunder	vermin	* partner	Cory	curfew
* enter	* under	Vermont	* party	distort	current
* finger	* verbal	versus	* target	endorse	curtsy
* gather	* whisper		carcass	escort	disturb
* hammer	* winter		carpet	export	flirted
* hunger	* zipper		darling	forbid	furnish
* ladder	adverb		discard	forceps	further
* lantern	berserk		farther	horrid	murder
* letter	butler		garlic	import	murmur
* lumber	chatter		garter	inform	occur
* manner	expert		hardly	morbid	perturb
* matter	fender		harness	mortal	squirrel
* member	hermit		harvest	orbit	squirted
* number	lobster		jargon	order	surplus
* offer	master		parcel	torment	surprise
* pepper	monster		pardon	orphan	turban
* perfect	pamper		parsnip	perform	turnip
* perfume	pattern		tardy		urban
* permit	perhaps				
* person	persist				
* rubber	Peter				
* sermon	rather				

Three-Syllable Words

* carpenter	* interrupt	Armando	turpentine
* different	abnormal	informal	
* important	Ariel	Lorenzo	

*Practical spelling words. The teacher and student should decide together how many of these words the student will be responsible for spelling.

TYPES OF SYLLABLES The *r*-Controlled Syllable (V*r*)

The **r-controlled syllable (Vr)** has a vowel followed by an *r*. The vowel sound is neither long nor short, but has its own sound.

➡ Learn these sounds.

ar	says /ar/ as in	*car*	
or	says /or/ as in	*fort*	
er	says /er/ as in	*fern*	⎫
ir	says /er/ as in	*bird*	⎬ These all have the same sound: /er/
ur	says /er/ as in	*church*	⎭

➡ Circle only those syllables below that are *r*-controlled syllables. Then copy them under the headings below according to their vowel-*r* sound. Read the syllables to another student.

vir	tle	lish	lum	nee	cass
tern	tar	thir	par	ber	bine
mit	poin	per	sume	turb	sorb
surd	sher	mur	squir	la	cir
gar	dar	vi	nor	tort	cort

/ar/ as in *car*

_____

_____

_____

/or/ as in *fort*

_____

_____

_____

/er/ as in *fern*

_____

_____

_____

/er/ as in *bird*

_____

_____

_____

/er/ as in *church*

_____

_____

_____

Review

A **closed syllable** has _____ vowel and ends in a _____.

A **silent-*e* syllable** has a vowel-_____-*e*.

An ***r*-controlled** syllable has a vowel followed by an _____.

A **closed syllable** has a _____ vowel sound.

A **silent-*e* syllable** has a _____ vowel sound.

Which syllable has neither a short- nor a long-vowel sound?_____

➤ Copy these syllables under the correct headings. Then read them to another student.

nish	tal	fen	ur	lete	cus
ler	tane	plode	es	mon	lide
cuse	ster	sist	lute	thun	tort
sur	trive	tern	car	pur	sume

Closed Syllables VC	Silent-*e* Syllables VC*e*	*r*-Controlled Syllables V*r*
_____	_____	_____
_____	_____	_____
_____	_____	_____
_____	_____	_____
_____	_____	_____
_____	_____	_____
_____	_____	_____

➡️ Your teacher will dictate ten *r*-controlled syllables for you to spell. Repeat the syllables aloud while spelling.

1. _____   6. _____

2. _____   7. _____

3. _____   8. _____

4. _____   9. _____

5. _____   10. _____

➡️ List the three possible spellings for the /er/ sound: _____, _____, _____. When spelling the /er/ sound in the syllables below, more than one spelling may be correct. You need to spell only one.

1. _____   5. _____   8. _____

2. _____   6. _____   9. _____

3. _____   7. _____ 10. _____

4. _____

➡️ Listen for the vowel sound in these dictated syllables. If you hear a short-vowel sound, spell the syllable under _____ Syllables. If you hear a long-vowel sound, spell the syllable under _____ Syllables. If you hear neither a short- nor a long-vowel sound, spell the syllable under _____ Syllables.

Closed Syllables	**Silent-*e* Syllables**	***r*-Controlled Syllables**
_____	_____	_____
_____	_____	_____
_____	_____	_____
_____	_____	_____
_____	_____	_____

➡ Mark the short vowels and combine the syllables to read the whole word. Circle the syllables as shown.

bŭt	ler	(but)(ler)
mur	mur	murmur
ad	verb	adverb
tur	ban	turban

sher	bet	sherbet
ab	surd	absurd
dis	turb	disturb
bur	den	burden

➡ Match the syllables to make a real word. Then say it as you write it.

per	cort _____	ham	vest _____
num	cus _____	squir	mer _____
cir	ber _____	har	form _____
es	haps _____	per	rel _____

gar	ster _____	car	surd _____
mon	rent _____	per	pet _____
mur	lic _____	tur	son _____
cur	mur _____	ab	nip _____

➡ Reorder the syllables to make a recognizable word.

por	im	tant	_____
in	rupt	ter	_____
ter	pen	car	_____
fer	dif	ent	_____
nor	mal	ab	_____
pen	tur	tine	_____
mal	for	in	_____

➤ *per* is a common spelling for the /per/ sound at the beginning of words. Fill in the missing syllable *per* and match the words to the definitions.

_____fume	1. allow to do something	_____
_____fect	2. maybe	_____
_____son	3. lasting	_____
_____mit	4. without fault	_____
_____haps	5. trouble greatly	_____
_____sist	6. sweet-smelling liquid	_____
_____turb	7. refuse to stop	_____
_____ma nent	8. man, woman, child	_____

➤ *ver* is a common spelling pattern in two-syllable words. Fill in the missing letters *ver* and match the words to the definitions.

_____sus	1. decision of a jury	_____
_____min	2. northeastern state	_____
_____dict	3. part of speech	_____
ad_____b	4. against	_____
_____mont	5. fleas, lice, rats, bedbugs	_____

➤ *tur* is a common spelling for the /ter/ sound in two-syllable words. Fill in the missing letters *tur* and match the words to the definitions.

_____nip	1. scarf worn around the head	_____
per_____b	2. used to thin paint	_____
_____ban	3. large bird	_____
dis_____b	4. trouble greatly	_____
_____key	5. root; type of vegetable	_____
_____pen tine	6. destroy peace and quiet	_____

➡ The /er/ sound at the end of words is most often spelled with *er*. Read the clues, spell the missing syllable using *er*, and then write the whole word. The first one is done for you.

1. talk softly   whis**per**_____   _whisper_____
2. a metal   sil_____   _____
3. comes after fall   win_____   _____
4. opposite of over   un_____   _____
5. to go in   en_____   _____
6. you have five on each hand   fin_____s   _____
7. a shellfish   lob_____   _____
8. part of a book   chap_____   _____
9. need for food   hun_____   _____
10. logs, boards   lum_____   _____
11. feeling mad   an_____   _____
12. 32 is one   num_____   _____
13. front part of a car fen_____   _____
14. state of mind   tem_____   _____
15. slim   slen_____   _____
16. noise heard in storms thun_____   _____
17. to bring together gath_____   _____

EXCEPTION   Practice these exceptions.

occur   murmur

occ __ __   murm __ __

o __ c __ r   m __ rm __ r

__ __ __ __ __   __ __ __ __ __ __

➡ Your teacher will dictate some words. Repeat the word, isolate the missing syllable, and spell it. Then write the whole word, saying it aloud as you spell.

1. _____ den   _____

2. _____ son   _____

3. _____ ner   _____

4. _____ ner   _____

5. _____ dict   _____

6. _____ key   _____

7. chap _____   _____

8. mur _____   _____

9. fur _____   _____

10. dis _____   _____

11. sil _____   _____

12. ex _____   _____

13. bar _____   _____

14. _____pen _____   _____

15. dif _____ ent   _____

16. im _____ tant   _____

Review

Match the syllable to its sign.

Closed Syllable	V*r*
Silent-*e* Syllable	VC
r-Controlled Syllable	VC*e*

➡ What is the VC/CV Syllabication Rule? _____

_____

★ Often the first syllable of a word has a short vowel sound because it is a closed syllable. Sometimes, however, the first syllable is *r*-controlled.

➡ Divide these words into syllables, mark the short vowels, and copy them by syllables into the boxes below.

enforce	burden	absurd	sherbet	verdict
jargon	different	abnormal	curfew	orbit
interrupt	turpentine	urban	berserk	informal
perturb	escort	absorb	important	carpenter
forceps				

Two-Syllable Words

Three-Syllable Words

Circle the *er, ur,* and *ir* r–controlled combinations in the following common words. Then write them under the correct heading

f(ur)th(er)	squirrel	disturb	interrupt	murmur
person	thunder	sermon	servant	permit
surprise	turkey	burden	differ	squirted
circus	perfume	hunger	furnish	whisper
perfect				

er **Words**	*ur* **Words**	*ir* **Words**
further	*further*	

Review

Three ways to spell the sound /er/ are _____, _____, and _____.

Have another student test you on spelling these common words.

My score: _____ words correct.

⭐ Usually, a short vowel in the first syllable of a multisyllabic word must be followed by two consonants. If you hear a single consonant sound between two vowels, you must remember to double the middle consonant.

➡ Can you figure out the following words? Say the syllables aloud as you spell the words.

1. not sweet, nor sour	bi __ __ er	_____
2. used to pound nails	ha __ __ er	_____
3. small animal that eats acorns	squi __ __ el	_____
4. comes after spring	su __ __ er	_____
5. evening meal	su __ __ er	_____
	di __ __ er	_____
6. spread on bread	bu __ __ er	_____
7. type of metal	co __ __ er	_____
8. used to climb	la __ __ er	_____
9. disagree	di __ __ er	_____
10. light, low shoe	sli __ __ er	_____
11. _____band	ru __ __ er	_____
12. to feel pain	su __ __ er	_____
13. mail	le __ __ er	_____
14. something that zips	zi __ __ er	_____
15. good, _____, best	be __ __ er	_____

➡ Have another student test you on spelling these common words.

My score: _____ words correct.

Review

The **VC/CV Syllabication Rule** says that when two or more consonants (C) stand between two vowels, you divide between the _____.

➡ To spell the /ən/ sound at the end of these words, you must choose between *on, an,* or *en.* Circle the *on, an,* or *en* in the following words. Then write them under the correct heading.

| *person | orphan | burden | *carbon | *sermon | pardon |
| jargon | *garden | urban | *organ | turban | |

an **Words**	*on* **Words**	*en* **Words**
_____	_____	_____
_____	_____	_____
_____	_____	
_____	_____	
	_____	

➡ To spell these words you must choose between *et* and *it.* Circle the *et* or *it* in the following words. Then write them under the correct heading.

| *market | hermit | *target | orbit | *permit | sherbet |

et **Words**	*it* **Words**
_____	_____
_____	_____
_____	_____

➡ Have another student test you on the starred words. They are practical spelling words.

My score: _____ words correct.

Proofing Practice

➡ Two common List 4 words are misspelled in each of the sentences below. Correct them as shown.

    carpenter's   *farmer's*

1. The ~~carpanter's~~ hammer, the ~~farmar's~~ rake, or the artist's knife could have been used to prop open the window.

2. Morris served lobster, bread with garlic buttor, and sherbet for super.

3. If the children wisper and chatter, they will disturb everyone at the orgen concert.

→ Here are more words from List 4 that you are likely to use in writing. Be sure that you learn how to spell these words. Fill in the blanks with words that make sense in the sentences.

partner	squirrels	correct	gather	chapter	furnish
further	order	barber	permit	lantern	perfect
matter	perfume	carpenter	organ	important	artist

1. Walter has to finish reading _____ five for history class tomorrow.

2. The wind was strong, so it was a _____ day to go sailing.

3. The _____ will cut your hair at 10:00 a.m.

4. How much _____ do we have to go?

5. My business _____ made an _____ sale today.

6. A building _____ is needed before a _____ can start to build a house.

7. _____ your things so we can leave now.

8. Doris smells nice. She is wearing a new kind of _____.

9. The _____ were making a lot of noise scampering from tree to tree.

10. Does it _____ if we're ten minutes late?

11. The _____ sold his paintings at the fair.

12. We want to _____ the house with new chairs. We will have to

    _____ them from the store.

13. The teacher has many tests to _____ before class.

14. Because it's so dark tonight, we should put a _____ out on the patio.

15. The class went to hear Victor play the _____ at the church.

➡ Select a word from below that can be used in place of the words that are underlined in the sentences. Write the correct word to the right of each sentence. Use your dictionary. Then complete the puzzle.

1. When I'm sick, I like to have someone <u>give lots of attention to</u> me.

   _____
   (6 down)

2. Carmen could hear the <u>soft, low sound</u> of voices in the next room.

   _____
   (9 across)

3. There is a great need for more <u>city</u> housing.

   _____
   (11 across)

4. Martin lives in a shack in the woods. People call him a <u>person who goes away from other people to live by himself</u>.

   _____
   (2 down)

5. Doctors use a lot of <u>special words</u> that most people don't understand.

   _____
   (5 down)

6. Ginger found the <u>dead body</u> of a deer in the forest.

   _____
   (8 across)

7. People are <u>beings that are sure to die sometime</u>.

   _____
   (10 across)

8. Norman's plan to hitchhike to Vermont is <u>foolish and unreasonable</u>.

   _____
   (1 down)

9. Victor had his arms filled with <u>packages and gifts</u>.

   _____
   (4 down)

10. Don't forget to <u>write your name on the back of</u> the check before you put it into the bank.

    _____
    (7 across)

11. These prank phone calls <u>greatly trouble</u> me.

    _____
    (6 across)

12. We found lots of <u>fleas, rats, and bugs</u> in the rundown shack.

    _____
    (3 down)

pamper	hermit	mortals	perturb	jargon	vermin
absurd	murmur	endorse	urban	carcass	parcels

51

➡ Read the following sentences and circle all the List 4 words that you can find.

1. During the summer, the weather is almost perfect in Vermont.

2. The jury reached a verdict of guilty in the murder case.

3. Walter will plant turnips and parsnips in his garden this year.

4. We must whisper so that we don't disturb the person in the next room.

5. The expert carpenter needs more lumber and a ladder before she builds the house.

6. The United States imports rubber and exports its surplus wheat.

7. Arnell will furnish the punch for the surprise dinner party.

8. The squirrel ran up the tree when the thunder started.

9. The lobster pinched the servant's finger.

10. Martin wants to order garlic bread for supper.

➡ Take out a piece of blank paper. Your teacher will dictate three of the sentences above for you to write.

➡ Now select ten words from List 4 and create a short story or a descriptive paragraph that uses those words. Be creative and avoid repetition!

Reading Accuracy: Demonstrate your accuracy in reading and spelling List 4 words. Your teacher will select ten words to read and ten practical spelling words for you to spell. Record your scores on the Accuracy Checklist. Work toward 90–100 percent accuracy.

Reading Proficiency: Now build up your reading fluency with List 4 words. Decide on your rate goal with your teacher. Record your progress on the Proficiency Graph.

My goal for reading List 4 is _____ words per minute with two or fewer errors.

LIST 5: V/CV SYLLABICATION RULE

/ā/	/ē/	/ī/	/ō/	/ū/ and /o͞o/
* agent	* even	* cider	* bonus	* duty
* bacon	* evil	* fiber	* donate	* pupil
* basic	* female	* final	* hotel	* student
* basin	* fever	* item	* local	* tulip
* crater	* frequent	* minus	* locate	* unite
* crazy	* legal	* pilot	* open	brutal
* label	* secret	* rival	* pony	Cuban
* lady	* veto	* siren	* solo	cupid
* later	decent	* spider	* spoken	human
* lazy	decide	* tiger	* total	humid
* paper	deduct	* vital	* trophy	music
* raven	demon	bison	holy	puny
baby	ego	climax	moment	putrid
blazer	elope	iris	omit	super
gravy	equal	Irish	poker	Susan
halo	erase	ivy	polo	tuna
Jason	event	lilac	rodent	tunic
navy	hero	silent	roman	unit
Stacey	meter	spiral	rotate	
vacant	recent	tidy	slogan	
	Steven	tiny	sloping	
	Venus	virus	sober	
	zero		toga	
			totem	
			Yoko	

*Practical spelling words. The teacher and the student should decide together how many of these words the student will be responsible for spelling.

TYPES OF SYLLABLES The Open Syllable (CV)

An **open syllable (CV)** ends in one vowel. The vowel is usually long (lō, crā).

Review

A **closed syllable (VC)** has one vowel, ends in a consonant, and has a short-vowel sound. (*trŏm, jĕct*).

A **silent-*e* syllable (VC*e*)** has one vowel followed by a consonant followed by an *e*.

The *e* is silent and makes the preceding vowel long (āce, hīde).

An ***r*-controlled syllable (V*r*)** has a vowel followed by an *r*, which changes the sound.

The sounds are: *ar* as in *car; ir, ur, er* as in *bird, church, fern;* and *or* as in *fort*.

➡ Write the following syllables in the correct columns.

la	ber	nus	lope	cate
ter	so	dent	tem	dy
ris	e	fi	per	ser
spo	vil	ru	lent	cret
male	rase	der	lite	nate

Open (CV)	Closed (VC)	Silent-*e* (VC*e*)	*r*-Controlled (V*r*)
_____	_____	_____	_____
_____	_____	_____	_____
_____	_____	_____	_____
_____	_____	_____	_____
_____	_____	_____	_____
_____	_____		
_____	_____		

➡ Now practice reading the syllables.

★ Your teacher will dictate nine syllables. Repeat the syllable and write it in the correct column.

Open (CV)	Closed (VC)	Silent-*e* (VC*e*)	*r*-Controlled (V*r*)
_____	_____	_____	_____
_____	_____	_____	
_____	_____		

RULE

The **V/CV Syllabication Rule:** When a single consonant is surrounded by two vowels, the most common division is before the consonant. The first syllable is open and the vowel sound is long.

➤ Mark the long vowels and combine the syllables to read the whole word. Divide the syllables as shown.

crā	zy	cra|zy
I	rish	Irish
fe	male	female
hu	man	human
ha	lo	halo
u	nit	unit

he	ro	hero
i	ris	iris
pu	ny	puny
cra	ter	crater
u	nite	unite
pi	lot	pilot

➤ Match the syllables to make a real word; then say it as you write it. The first one is done for you.

i	ven	_____
ra	vy	_ivy_
e	mid	_____
hu	ven	_____

bru	bot	_____
le	tal	_____
ba	con	_____
ro	gal	_____

e	nal	_____
va	ber	_____
fi	vil	_____
so	cant	_____

se	pid	_____
stu	ver	_____
slo	gan	_____
fe	cret	_____

➤ Complete the definitions with one of these words: open, silent-*e*, *r*-controlled, closed.

An _____ syllable ends in one vowel. The vowel is usually long.

A _____ syllable has one vowel, ends in a consonant, and has a short-vowel sound.

➡ Your teacher will dictate twelve words. Listen carefully and fill in the missing syllable, sounding it out as you write. Then write the whole word.

1. _____ ven   _____

2. _____ zy   _____

3. _____ cate   _____

4. _____ ty   _____

5. _____ nal   _____

6. po _____   _____

7. bo _____   _____

8. fe _____   _____

9. la _____   _____

10. spi _____   _____

11. fe _____   _____

12. ho _____   _____

Review the Rules

The **V/CV Syllabication Rule:** When a single c_____ is surrounded by two

v_____, the most common division is before the c_____. This makes

the first syllable o_____ and the vowel sound l_____.

➡ Fill in the blank with the sign for each type of consonant. Choose the sign from this list:

CV, VC*e*, VC, V*r*

r-Controlled Syllable _____

Closed Syllable _____

Open Syllable _____

Silent-*e* Syllable _____

★ Many V/CV words have a schwa sound /ə/ in the second syllable. The second syllable has the schwa sound because it is unaccented. The accent is usually on the first syllable of two-syllable words. Learn these schwa ending patterns found in V/CV words.

➤ *al* is a common way to spell the /əl/ sound at the end of some V/CV words. Read the definitions to figure out the words below. Write the missing syllable using *al* and then write the whole world.

1. at the end; the last   *fi __ __ __   _____

2. having to do with a certain place   *lo __ __ __   _____

3. the same amount   e __ __ __ __   _____

4. cruel, like a brute   bru __ __ __   _____

5. having to do with the law   *le __ __ __   _____

6. one who tries to outdo another   *ri __ __ __   _____

7. whole; entire   *to __ __ __   _____

8. a winding coil   spi __ __ __   _____

9. having to do with life   *vi __ __ __   _____

➤ Practice spelling the common exceptions:

*la bel   *e vil   *pu pil

la b __ __   ev __ __   pu p __ __

l __ b __ __   __ v __ __   p __ p __ __

__ __ __ __ __   __ __ __ __   __ __ __ __ __

➤ *ent* is often used to spell the the /ənt/ sound at the end of some V/CV words. Add *ent* to these common words and then spell the whole word.

*a g __ __ __   _____   re c __ __ __   _____

*fre qu __ __ __   _____   si l __ __ __   _____

*stu d __ __ __   _____   ro d __ __ __   _____

➤ Have another student test you on spelling the starred words. They are practical spelling words.

My score: _____ words correct.

Review

When you hear the /ən/ sound at the end of two-syllable words, you will usually choose one of these spellings:

Choice #1	*on*	as in *ribbon*
Choice #2	*en*	as in *kitten*
Choice #3	*in*	as in *napkin*
Choice #4	*an*	as in *urban*

➡ Circle the last two letters in each of the following V/CV words. Then write the words under the correct headings.

*even	*basin	*open	demon
*human	slogan	bison	siren
*spoken	*bacon	*raven	Susan

on

_____

_____

_____

en

_____

_____

_____

_____

in

_____

an

_____

_____

_____

➡ The /əd/ sound at the end of words is sometimes spelled *id*. Read the definitions to figure out the missing syllable. Then write the whole word.

1. smells bad; rotten   put __ __ __   _____

2. hot and muggy   hu __ __ __   _____

3. god of love   Cu __ __ __   _____

➡️ These words follow the V/CV Syllabication Rule. The first vowel ends the first syllable and is long. The second vowel may be schwa, long, short, silent-*e*, or *r*-controlled. The accent is on the first syllable of these words and of most two-syllable words.

Divide between the syllables and mark the first vowel long as shown. Write the word by syllables, putting the first (accented) syllable in the box and the second (unaccented) syllable in the blank.

Then complete the puzzle.

basin   `ba`   `sin`
(13 Down)

hero
(3 Across)

tidy
(12 Down)

total
(6 Across)

cupid
(15 Across)

slogan
(2 Down)

meter
(8 Across)

brutal
(7 Down)

pilot
(11 Across)

locate
(4 Across)

totem
(6 Down)

equal
(9 Across)

crater
(15 Down)

legal
(16 Across)

basic
(1 Across)

evil
(5 Down)

lazy
(14 Across)

unit
(10 Down)

In the words above, the first syllable is always _____ and the vowel sound is always _____.

➤ Because any vowel can make the schwa sound, it is hard to know which vowel to use when spelling. Sometimes one way "looks right," and other ways "look funny." Circle the spelling that looks right to you. Then check your answers at the bottom of the page. If you are not sure, check right away. We don't want you getting used to the wrong way! Then write the correct spelling.

1. bacan
   bacon   _____
   bacen

2. pilot
   pilet   _____
   pilit

3. total
   totel   _____
   totil

4. humin
   humen   _____
   human

5. unet
   unit   _____
   unot

6. label
   labil   _____
   labal

7. secrit
   secrot   _____
   secret

8. final
   finel   _____
   finil

9. itum
   itim   _____
   item

10. evon
    evin   _____
    even

11. open
    opan   _____
    opin

12. frequant
    frequent _____
    frequint

When writing a word, if one way looks wrong, try another vowel.

➤ Have another student test you on these words. They are practical spelling words.

My score: _____ words correct.

Right way: bacon, pilot, total, human, unit, label, secret, final, item, even, open, frequent

➡ Your teacher will dictate ten common words. Write each word syllable-by-syllable on the lines provided, sounding it out as you write. Then write the whole word on the third line.

Sample: | lo | cal | local

1. _____

2. _____

3. _____

4. _____

5. _____ | _____ |

6. _____

7. _____

8. _____

9. _____

10. _____

Fill in the blanks with the correct words.

lilac	music	decide	tuna	super
Navy	tulip	solo	local	basic
cider	trophy	rotate	deduct	event
iris	crater	poker	secret	agent

1. A lake had formed in the _____ of the volcano.

2. Lucy can _____ the cost of child care when she pays her taxes.

3. The wedding of Stacey and Steven was a splendid _____.

4. The earth _____s on its axis.

5. Susan was a good card player. She got a _____ for winning the

   _____ game.

6. Since the _____ store does not have any apple

   _____, we will have to drive to one farther away.

7. Ruby bought _____ fish at the _____ market.

8. In the school's _____ program, Rosa sang a

   _____.

9. Yoko and Dale joined the _____ and took

   _____ training together.

10. I cannot _____ which flower I like best – the

    _____, the _____, or the

    _____.

11. James Bond is a _____ _____ who often deals

    with spies.

➡ Fill in the blanks with the correct words from the list below.

1. opposite of gentleman   _____

2. opposite of good   _____

3. opposite of include   _____

4. opposite of big   _____

5. opposite of closed   _____

6. opposite of noisy, loud   _____

7. opposite of odd   _____

8. opposite of sooner   _____

9. opposite of kind, gentle   _____

10. opposite of teacher   _____

11. opposite of male   _____

12. opposite of messy   _____

13. opposite of hard-working   _____

14. opposite of flat, even   _____

15. opposite of plus   _____

pupil	evil	tidy	brutal	sloping
omit	female	open	lazy	minus
even	tiny	lady	silent	later

Proofing Practice

➡ Two common List 5 words are misspelled in each of the sentences below. Correct them as shown.

                              fever
1. The vet on duty said that high ~~feaver~~ and a virus caused the tigger's death.

2. The secret ajent tried to locait the legal papers in the forest.

3. How many itums will you donate to the lokal music fund sale?

4. Stacey put a lable on each iris and toolip in the tidy garden.

➡ Read the following sentences and circle all the List 5 words that you can find.

1. The Romans often wore togas and tunics.

2. At the zoo, Jason saw a pony, three tigers, and four bison.

3. The secret agent spent the night in the tiny hotel.

4. Cupid and Venus are the god and goddess of love.

5. The hotel clerk is not on duty tonight because he has a virus and a fever.

6. Owen read about an Irish hero.

7. Ten minus ten equals zero.

8. The label was printed on silver paper.

9. The baby would stop crying the moment we played music.

10. Lucy will donate some cash to her best music students.

11. Can the president veto the bill on equal rights?

➡ Take out a piece of blank paper. Your teacher will dictate three of the sentences above for you to write.

➡ Now select ten words from List 5 and create a short story or a descriptive paragraph that uses those words. Be creative and avoid repetition!

Reading Accuracy: Demonstrate your accuracy in reading and spelling List 5 words. Your teacher will select ten words to read and ten practical spelling words for you to spell. Record your scores on the Accuracy Checklist. Work toward 90–100 percent accuracy.

Reading Proficiency: Now build up your reading fluency with List 5 words. Decide on your rate goal with your teacher. Record your progress on the Proficiency Graph.

My goal for reading List 5 is _____ words per minute with two or fewer errors.

/ă/	/ĕ/	/ĭ/	/ŏ/	/ŭ/
* cabin	* clever	* finish	* body	* study
* dragon	* credit	* limit	* closet	punish
* habit	* ever	* linen	* copy	
* magic	* lemon	* mimic	* model	
* panel	* level	* prison	* modern	
* planet	* melon	* river	* novel	
* radish	* menu	* silver	* product	
* rapid	* metal	* timid	* proper	
* salad	* method	* visit	* robin	
* travel	* never	civic	* solid	
* vanish	* pedal	tribune	comet	
* wagon	* present	tribute	comic	
Andrew	* relish	vivid	frolic	
atom	* second	widow	John	
camel	* seven		Josh	
static	denim		Monica	
talent	desert		polish	
valid	devil		project	
	rebel		tonic	
	relic		topic	
	tepid		tropic	
			volume	

*Practical spelling words. The teacher and student should decide together how many of these words the student will be responsible for spelling.

Review

Review the types of syllables:

1. A *closed syllable* has one _____. It _____ in a consonant.

2. A *silent-e syllable* has a _____ – _____ – _____ pattern.

3. An *r-controlled syllable* has a vowel _____ by an *r*.

4. An *open syllable* _____ in one vowel.

5. Which two types of syllables have long-vowel sounds? _____ and

    _____

➤ Copy these syllables under the correct headings. Then read them to another student.

meth	ish	mod	ute	u
ume	nov	per	ny	une
ern	er			

Open (CV)	Closed (VC)	Silent-*e* (VC*e*)	*r*-Controlled (V*r*)
_____	_____	_____	_____
_____	_____	_____	_____
	_____	_____	
	_____		

➤ Your teacher will dictate ten syllables. Repeat the syllable and write it in the correct column.

Open (CV)	Closed (VC)	Silent-*e* (VC*e*)	*r*-Controlled (V*r*)
_____	_____	_____	_____
_____	_____	_____	_____
_____	_____		

RULE

The **VC/V Syllabication Rule:** Where a single consonant is surrounded by two vowels, try the V/CV Syllabication Rule first. If that doesn't make a recognizable word, divide after the consonant and give the first vowel its short sound.

➡ Mark the first vowel short and combine the syllables to read the whole word. Circle the syllables as shown.

tăl	ent	(tal)(ent)
at	om	atom
pun	ish	punish
trib	une	tribune
meth	od	method

lev	el	level
vol	ume	volume
cop	y	copy
dev	il	devil
rel	ic	relic

➡ Match the syllables to make a real word. Then say the word aloud as you write it.

trav	et	_closet_
rel	el	_____
stud	ish	_____
clos	y	_____

pun	el	_____
sol	im	_____
den	id	_____
pan	ish	_____

sal	on	_____
lem	ic	_____
prop	ad	_____
com	er	_____

riv	ume	_____
top	er	_____
vol	u	_____
men	ic	_____

sec	id	_____
ped	ond	_____
pol	al	_____
tim	ish	_____

plan	ish	_____
cop	el	_____
van	et	_____
nov	y	_____

→ *el* is a common spelling for the /əl/ sound at the end of words. Fill in the blanks with *el*, copy the whole word, and then arrange the words in alphabetical order.

Add *el*	Copy	ABC Order
*cam_____	_____	_____
*trav_____	_____	_____
*pan_____	_____	_____
*lev_____	_____	_____
reb_____	_____	_____
*mod_____	_____	_____
*nov_____	_____	_____

→ Practice these words that end in *al*.

*met al	met _____	_____	_____
*ped al	ped _____	_____	_____

→ *er* is the most common spelling for the /er/ sound at the end of the word. Fill in the blank with *er*, copy the whole word, and then arrange the words in alphabetical order.

Add *er*	Copy	ABC Order
*sliv _____	_____	_____
*nev _____	_____	_____
*clev _____	_____	_____
*riv _____	_____	_____
*ev _____	_____	_____
*prop _____	_____	_____

→ Have another student test you on spelling the starred words. They are practical spelling words.

My score: _____ words correct.

➤ *ic* and *ish* are common word endings found in VC/V words. Add the final syllable *ic* or *ish* to the syllables below to make a real word. Copy and then match the words to the definitions.

com _____   _____   van _____   _____

fin_____   _____   frol _____   _____

top _____   _____   rad _____   _____

pol _____   _____   stat _____   _____

mim _____   _____   pun _____   _____

ton _____   _____   mag _____   _____

clin_____   _____   civ_____   _____

1. copy; make fun of   * _____

2. of a city   _____

3. a drink that gives strength   _____

4. have fun; a merry game   _____

5. funny   * _____

6. cause pain or loss to someone   * _____

7. place to get medical help   _____

8. subject to think, write, or talk about   _____

9. at rest; standing still; noise in a radio broadcast   _____

10. end   * _____

11. disappear   * _____

12. unexplained   * _____

13. to make shiny   _____

14. red vegetable   * _____

➤ Have another student test you on spelling the starred words. They are practical spelling words.

My score: _____ words correct.

➡ Your teacher will dictate sixteen words. Repeat the word, isolate the missing syllable, and spell it. Then write the whole word, saying it aloud as you spell.

1. _____er   _____

2. _____on   _____

3. _____it   _____

4. trav_____   _____

5. _____al   _____

6. men_____   _____

7. _____ern   _____

8. rad_____   _____

9. _____in   _____

10. _____y   _____

11. bod_____   _____

12. _____id   _____

13. _____ad   _____

14. clev_____   _____

15. _____on   _____

16. mim_____   _____

➡ Choose any five of the words above and use them in sentences.

_____

_____

_____

_____

_____

_____

The **VC/V Syllabication Rule:** When a single consonant is surrounded by two vowels, try the V/CV Syllabication Rule first. If that doesn't make a recognizable word, divide after the consonant and give the first vowel its short sound.

➡ Directions:

VCV

1. Outline the vowels in red.
2. Place a dot just before the second vowel.
3. Draw an arc underneath the syllables.
4. Mark the vowels with a long (–), schwa (ə), or short (˘) sign.
5. Read the words to your teacher or another student.
6. Then complete the puzzle.

rằpĭd (17 Down)

menu (2 Down)

tribute (10 Down)

study (9 Across)

denim (18 Across)

volume (8 Down)

wagon (15 Across)

rebel (13 Across)

vanish (4 Down)

copy (3 Down)

visit (5 Down)

melon (11 Down)

atom (1 Across)

frolic (7 Down)

limit (12 Across)

credit (16 Across)

salad (14 Down)

punish (6 Across)

In the following words, you will have to decide whether to divide the word before the consonant (V/CV Syllabication Rule) or after it (VC/V Syllabication Rule). Divide and then pronounce the word as you write it under the correct heading. Mark the first vowel long or short.

V/CV		VC/V
lī|lac	lily lilac	lĭl|y
_____	secret second	_____
_____	even ever	_____
_____	punish puny	_____
_____	study student	_____
_____	final finish	_____
_____	meter metal	_____
_____	polo polish	_____

Review

When you hear the /ən/ sound at the end of two-syllable words, you will usually use one of these spellings:

Choice #1	*on*	as in	*ribbon*
Choice #2	*en*	as in	*kitten*
Choice #3	*in*	as in	*napkin*
Choice #4	*an*	as in	*urban*

➤ Circle the last two letters in each of the following words. The write them under the correct heading.

dragon   wagon   melon   lemon   prison

cabin   seven   robin   linen

on	**en**	**in**
_____	_____	_____
_____	_____	_____
_____		
_____		
_____		

➤ Fill in the blanks with some of the words above so that the story makes sense.

Puff was a magic _____ who loved to eat fruit, especially

_____s and _____s. One day, he visited our

_____ in the woods, pulling a little red _____

behind him. He was wearing a blue hat and a _____ shirt that had

_____ buttons up the front.

➤ Have another student test you on spelling these practical spelling words.

My score: _____ words correct.

➤ To spell the /ət/ sound at the end of a two-syllable word, you must choose between *et* and *it*. Circle the *et* or *it* in the following words; then write them under the correct heading.

*habit   *planet   *visit   *closet   *limit   *credit

et Words	*it* Words
_____	_____
_____	_____
	_____
	_____

➤ The /əd/ sound at the end of words is sometimes spelled *id*. Add *id* to these words and match then to the definitions.

*rap _____   1. slightly warm   _____

*tim _____   2. true   _____

tep _____   3. quick, speedy   _____

val _____   4. hard, firm   _____

*sol _____   5. shy   _____

➤ Learn to spell these common exceptions:

*salad   *method

sal __ d   meth __ d

__ al __ d   __ eth __ d

s __ l __ __   m __ th __ __

__ __ __ __ __   __ __ __ __ __ __

➤ Have another student test you on spelling the starred words. They are practical spelling words.

My score: _____ words correct.

➡ Here are some words from List 6 that you are likely to use in writing. Be sure you learn how to spell these words. Fill in the blanks with words that make sense in the sentences.

present	modern	copy	body	vanish
second	product	method	salad	visit
level	magic	solid	study	robin

1. Andrew and Adam would like to share a _____ for lunch.

2. Lashonda has to stay home and _____ tonight for a math test.

3. It is the best _____ we have on the market. You should buy it without

   a _____ thought.

4. I would rather live in a more _____ house. Old homes tend to have too many problems.

5. I like the way Josh teaches music. He uses the latest _____.

6. The top shelf is not _____. Can you make it flat?

7. They were glad to leave the boat and put their feet on _____ ground.

8. Kevin knows a lot of _____ tricks.

9. Do you mind if I make a _____ of that photo? I would like to send one to Monica.

10. John has a strong healthy _____. He makes an effort to keep fit.

11. Enrique's birthday is next week. I need to buy him a _____.

12. The _____ is one of the first birds seen in spring.

13. The rabbit seemed to _____ as the magician waved his scarf.

14. We were allowed to _____ him at the hospital.

Select a word from the bottom of the page that can be used in place of the words that are underlined in the sentences. Write the correct word to the right of each sentence. Use your dictionary.

1. Last night we saw a <u>star-like body with a tail of light</u> streak through the sky.

    _____

2. Thomas had a <u>factual, true</u> point to make about the new tax laws.

    _____

3. The <u>foot lever</u> on my bike is broken.

    _____

4. A rose has many <u>colored leaves</u>.

    _____

5. This uniform is an <u>old object</u> from the Civil War.

    _____

6. Cod-liver oil is a <u>strength giving substance</u>; it contains vitamins A and D.

    _____

7. Andrew would like to take a cruise to the <u>hottest part of the earth around the equator</u>.

    _____

8. Memorial Day is a <u>way of showing respect and thanks</u> to our dead soldiers.

    _____

9. Helen Edison is a <u>woman whose husband is dead</u>.

    _____

10. Josh has a <u>new</u> plan for raising money for the clinic.

    _____

11. The <u>cubic space</u> of the fish tank is ten gallons.

    _____

12. Monica has some new jeans made from <u>a heavy cotton cloth</u>.

    _____

petals	widow	volume	tonic	relic	tropics
denim	comet	novel	tribute	pedal	valid

Two common List 6 words are misspelled in each of the sentences below. Correct them as shown.

    never

1. Janet had ~~nevver~~ traveled by camel before her second visit to the dessert.

2. For our class project, we will studdy Halley's comet and make a modle of it.

3. Thomas is clevor to write both novvels and comic book scripts.

4. The moddern, split-level house had no linen clozet.

➡ Read the following sentences and circle all the List 6 words that you can find.

1. Monica will order a large lemon wedge to go with the fresh melon.

2. Adam would like to get a copy of that book for a friend in prison.

3. Megan just read a clever novel about a magic dragon.

4. John never finds the time to polish his boots.

5. It was his habit to read comic books rather than to study his lessons.

6. Andrew put a radish in his fresh garden salad.

7. It must have been hard to travel across the desert in a covered wagon.

8. There are lots of rapids in the river by our cabin.

9. The comet streaked past the planet and then vanished from sight.

10. You can find a more modern product on the second level.

11. Josh hid Enrique's present in his bedroom closet.

➡ Take out a piece of blank paper. Your teacher will dictate three of the sentences above for you to write.

➡ Now select ten words from List 6 and create a short story or a descriptive paragraph that uses those words. Be creative and avoid repetition!

Reading Accuracy: Demonstrate your accuracy in reading and spelling List 6 words. Your teacher will select ten words to read and ten practical spelling words for you to spell. Record your scores on the Accuracy Checklist. Work toward 90–100 percent accuracy.

Reading Proficiency: Now build up your reading fluency with List 6 words. Decide on your rate goal with your teacher. Record your progress on the Proficiency Graph.

My goal for reading List 6 is _____ words per minute with two or fewer errors.

* apple	* little	* table	gurgle	riddle
* turtle	* marble	* uncle	hassle	ruffle
* able	* middle	* whistle	huddle	sample
* ankle	* muscle	* kettle	humble	simple
* battle	* needle	bridle	hustle	sparkle
* bottle	* purple	brittle	maple	stifle
* bundle	* puzzle	bugle	measles	stumble
* castle	* rattle	cable	noble	temple
* cattle	* rifle	candle	paddle	thimble
* circle	* saddle	crinkle	pebble	tremble
* cradle	* settle	crumble	people	trifle
* gentle	* single	cycle	pimple	twinkle
* handle	* sprinkle	eagle	poodle	wrestle
* idle	* stable	fable	puddle	

Three-Syllable Words

* example

  article

  icicle

  miracle

  particle

*Practical spelling words. The teacher and student should decide together how many of these words the student will be responsible for spelling.

TYPES OF SYLLABLES   The Double-vowel Syllable (VV) and the Consonant-*le* Syllable (C*le*)

A **double-vowel syllable (VV)** has two vowels that together make one sound. The sound has to be learned.

A **C*le* syllable (C*le*)** is a final syllable. The *e* is silent and the syllable sounds like consonant-/əl/ (ta*ble*, jun*gle*).

Review

An **open syllable (CV)** ends in one vowel. The vowel is usually long (lō, crā).

A **closed syllable (VC)** has one vowel, ends in a consonant, and has a short-vowel sound (trŏm, jĕct).

An **r-controlled syllable (Vr)** has a vowel followed by an *r*, which changes the sound of the vowel.

➡ Write the following syllables in the correct columns.

ple	mar	fle	kle	poo	pur
cra	dle	trem	bot	i	mea
am	gle	cir	mus	ket	mir
gur	un	bi	ea	nee	tle

Consonant-*le* (C*le*)	Double-Vowel (VV)	Open (CV)	Closed (VC)	r-Controlled (Vr)
_____	_____	_____	_____	_____
_____	_____	_____	_____	_____
_____	_____	_____	_____	_____
_____	_____		_____	_____
_____			_____	_____
_____			_____	

➡ Now practice reading the syllables.

➡ Your teacher will dictate five consonant-*le* syllables. Repeat each syllable and write it.

1. _____   2. _____   3. _____   4. _____   5. _____

RULE

The **Consonant-*le* Syllabication Rule (C*le*)** — When a word ends in a consonant-*le*, divide just before it. Count back three letters from the end of the word and divide.

➤ Pronounce and combine the syllables; then read the whole word.

sta	ble	stā|ble
pud	dle	puddle
ea	gle	eagle
pur	ple	purple
i	dle	idle

sam	ple	sample
bu	gle	bugle
ruf	fle	ruffle
bri	dle	bridle
cir	cle	circle

➤ Now look over the words. Mark between the syllables with a slash. Underline the consonant-*le* syllable. If the first syllable has a long or short vowel, mark it as shown above.

➤ Match the syllables to make a real word. Then say it as you write.

ri	ple _____		pim	dle _____
poo	tle _____		cra	ple _____
tem	fle _____		gur	ble _____
gen	dle _____		stum	gle _____
brit	ple _____		twin	tle _____
hud	ble _____		bat	kle _____
sta	dle _____		bu	dle _____
pur	tle _____		nee	gle _____

➤ Unscramble these three-syllable words.

am	ple	ex	_____
ti	ar	cle	_____
cle	a	mir	_____
i	cle	ci	_____

➤ Your teacher will dictate twenty words. Listen carefully and fill in the missing syllable, sounding it aloud as you spell. Then write the whole word, saying it as you write.

1. _____ ple _____

2. _____ gle _____

3. _____ dle _____

4. _____ dle _____

5. _____ tle _____

6. _____ ble _____

7. _____ ble _____

8. _____ dle _____

9. _____ dle _____

10. _____ dle _____

11. ri_____ _____

12. peo_____ _____

13. puz_____ _____

14. bat_____ _____

15. ea_____ _____

16. mid_____ _____

17. gur_____ _____

18. cir_____ _____

19. ta_____ _____

20. ruf_____ _____

➤ Make a word by adding one of the following consonant-*le* syllables. Then write the whole word, saying it as you write.

ble **dle** **tle** **fle** **kle**

1. star_____ _____

2. pad_____ _____

3. sta_____ _____

4. cat_____ _____

5. ca_____ _____

6. tur_____ _____

7. sad_____ _____

8. ta_____ _____

9. spar_____ _____

10. twin_____ _____

11. han_____ _____

12. mar_____ _____

13. bot_____ _____

14. bat_____ _____

15. fa_____ _____

16. raf_____ _____

17. poo_____ _____

18. han_____ _____

19. sprin_____ _____

20. cra_____ _____

➡ Sometimes the consonant in a *Cle* pattern is silent. *tle* and *cle* are sometimes pronounced /əl/. Add *tle* or *cle* to the following letters to make a word. Then write the whole word, saying it as you write.

hus_____   _____   wres_____   _____

*cas_____   _____   *whis_____   _____

*mus____   _____

Fill in the blanks with one of the above words.

The king and the queen live in one. _____

To work rapidly with energy. _____

The tissue in our bodies that lets us move. _____

To compete on a mat with another person. _____

This is a sound we can make with our mouth and lips. _____

➡ There are two ways to spell the /kəl/ sound: *cle* as in <u>un</u><u>cle</u> and *kle* as in *an<u>kle</u>*.

Circle *kle* or *cle* in the following words. Then write them under the right heading.

crinkle   *ankle   *circle

*sprinkle   sparkle   cycle

*uncle   twinkle

kle	**cle**
_____	_____
_____	_____
_____	_____
_____	
_____	

➡ Have another student test you on spelling the starred words. They are practical spelling words.

My score: _____ words correct.

➡ These words follow the /Cle Syllabication Rule. They are divided just before the Cle. The accent is on the first syllable of these words and of most two-syllable words.

Divide between the syllables and mark the first vowel. Draw a line though the silent e at the end of each word. Write the word by syllables, putting the first (accented) syllable in the box and the second (unaccented) syllable in the blank.

pĕbblé	peb	ble	idle		_____
huddle		_____	noble		_____
puddle		_____	circle		_____
bugle		_____	riddle		_____
stable		_____	gurgle		_____
poodle		_____	cable		_____
sample		_____	stumble		_____
uncle		_____	tremble		_____
purple		_____	cattle		_____

In the words above, the final syllable is always a _____ syllable.

➡ Divide the following words into syllables. Then categorize them according to the first syllable.

cra|dle	circle	measles
needle	purple	able
cattle	poodle	marble
humble	puddle	sample
sparkle	temple	stable
rifle	idle	steeple

Closed	*Cle*
_____	_____
_____	_____
_____	_____
_____	_____
_____	_____

r-Controlled	*Cle*
_____	_____
_____	_____
_____	_____

Open	*Cle*
cra	dle
_____	_____
_____	_____
_____	_____

Double-Vowel	*Cle*
_____	_____
_____	_____
_____	_____

➤ Your teacher will dictate sixteen words. If the first syllable has a long-vowel sound, write the word under the Open/Cle column. If the first syllable has a short-vowel sound, write the word under the Closed/Cle column and be sure to double the middle consonant.

Open / Cle
tā / ble

1. _____
2. _____
3. _____
4. _____
5. _____
6. _____
7. _____

Closed / Cle
ăp / ple

1. _____
2. _____
3. _____
4. _____
5. _____
6. _____
7. _____
8. _____
9. _____

➤ These common words have silent letters. Cross out the silent letters and then practice spelling them.

people

pe __ pl __

p __ __ p __ e

— — — — — —

whistle

w __ is __ le

__ __ i __ __ le

— — — — — — —

muscle

mus __ le

mu __ __ le

— — — — — —

➡️ Fill in each box with one of the words from the bottom of the page.

Consonant-*le*

1. not working; lazy

2. a big bird; the U.S. symbol

3. between the foot and leg

4. a story with a lesson

5. a kind of horn used in the army

6. make a bubbling noise

7. to crowd together

8. to stop the breath of; smother

9. not proud

10. a strip of gathered cloth

11. used on your finger for sewing

12. easily broken

13. a wonderful happening; almost magic

14. a sample; a model

15. a written part of a book or magazine

ankle	brittle	bugle	example	huddle
gurgle	article	stifle	idle	ruffle
humble	eagle	thimble	fable	miracle

Proofing Practice

➡️ Two common List 7 words are misspelled in each of the sentences below. Correct them as shown.

1. I wish that your poodle would ~~settel~~ *settle* down instead of running around in curcles.

2. The purple glass bottel sparkled on the marbble table.

3. Joel sprinkled pebbles in the puddle so the littel tertle could sit on them.

4. If you put a handdle on the middle bundle, you'll be abel to carry it.

➡ Here are some words from List 7 that you are likely to use in writing. Be sure you learn how to spell these words. Fill in the blanks with words that make sense in the sentences.

purple	handle	apples	uncle	marbles	simple
ankle	circle	needle	turtle	middle	kettle
people	twinkle	single	able	sprinkle	eagle

1. Jamal sprained his _____ when he was picking

   _____ off the tree.

2. Do you want a _____ or double scoop of ice cream?

3. _____ the goblets with care.

4. My _____ will not be _____ to attend the
   family picnic. He is going to be out of town.

5. Grandma will sew your pants if you bring her the _____ and thread.

6. Draw a big _____ in the _____ of your paper.

7. Many _____ like to look at the stars and watch them _____.

8. Robert wants to play a game of _____ with his friend.

9. A _____ is a reptile that has a hard outer shell.

10. It hasn't rained for awhile. We should _____ the garden with water.

11. The color _____ is made by mixing red and blue.

12. Polly put the _____ on; we'll all have tea.

13. The bald _____ is a magnificent bird.

14. This arithmetic problem is quite _____.

➡ Find and circle the eighteen words above in the puzzle below. The words can be found in a straight line or across or up and down.

```
A P P L E S M A R B L E S D A N E H P U R P L E
B E I S P R I N K L E M I D D L E H A N D L E A
L N N T W I N K L E S N E L W E C I R C L E I G
E S D S I N G L E T U R T L E N E E D L E S H L
S I M P L E K E T T L E P I P E O P L E R S A E
```

87

➡ Read the following sentences and circle all the List 7 words that you can find.

1. I could not decide whether he had pimples or the measles.
2. Megan took the saddle and bridle back to the stable.
3. Martin was so little that he didn't have enough muscle to wrestle on the team.
4. The tailor got out his needle, thread, and thimble and sewed a ruffle on Jill's dress.
5. The eagle landed in the maple tree near a castle.
6. After the baby had her bottle, she gurgled a little, and then slept in the cradle.
7. My uncle would rather play marbles than do a puzzle.
8. Be gentle with the little poodle.
9. Lucy stumbled over the pebbles and sprained her ankle.
10. Did you read the article about the miracle drug?
11. Most people like peanut brittle.

➡ Look at List 7. Choose five words and write them in sentences below.

_____

_____

_____

_____

_____

➡ Take out a piece of blank paper. Your teacher will dictate three of the sentences above for you to write.

You have completed the worksheets for List 7. Now it is time to check your accuracy in reading and spelling. Read and spell ten words selected by your teacher, and record your scores on the Accuracy Checklist. Work toward 90–100 percent accuracy.

When you have achieved 90–100 percent accuracy in reading, build up your reading speed. Decide on your rate goal with your teacher. Record your rate on the Proficiency Graph.

My goal for reading List 7 is _____ words per minute with two or fewer errors.

LIST 8: V/V SYLLABICATION RULE

/ā/	/ē/	/ī/	/ō/	/ū/ and /ōō/
chaos	* create	* dial	* poem	* cruel
chaotic	* idea	* diet	* poet	* duel
	* real	* lion	boa	* fuel
	cameo	* quiet	coerce	continuum
	ideal	* science	Noel	duet
	meander	* trial	oasis	fluent
	museum	client		fluid
	neon	defiant		influence
	nucleus	Diana		minuet
	react	iodine		ruin
	rodeo	iota		suet
	Romeo	Iowa		truant
		pioneer		
		riot		
		triumph		
		violence		
		violent		
		violet		
		violin		

*Practical spelling words. The teacher and student should decide together how many of these words the student will be responsible for spelling.

Review

Before learning about the V/V Syllabication Rule, it is neccesary to review double vowels (VV) so that you can learn to tell the two patterns apart.

Double-Vowel Syllables (VV) have two vowels that together make one sound. These sounds must be learned.

➤ Circle the double vowels in the following words. Remember that *y* and *w* sometimes act as vowels. Then write the words under the headings according to their vowel sounds.

flies	clay	fruit	yellow
brief	doe	grew	sleigh
pay	team	break	goal
coast	moose	grow	lie
meal	seed	rain	group
blue	die	spies	tree

/ā/ sound   **/ē/ sound**   **/ō/ sound**

_____   _____   _____

_____   _____   _____

_____   _____   _____

_____   _____   _____

_____   _____   _____

/ī/ sound   **/ū/ or /o͞o/ sound**

_____   _____   _____

_____   _____   _____

_____   _____   _____

➡ Circle the double vowels in the following words. Then write them under the headings according to their special vowel sounds.

crawl	mouse	shout
broil	town	oink
took	meant	taught
bread	haul	stood
joy	brook	health
sauce	boy	round

/aw/ as in *saw*

_____

_____

_____

_____

/ow/ as in *cow*

_____

_____

_____

_____

/oi/ as in *oil*

_____

_____

_____

_____

/ŏŏ/ as in *look*

_____

_____

_____

/ĕ/ as in *head*

_____

_____

_____

Review

Double-vowel syllables (VV) have _____ vowels that together make one sound.

The /aw/ sound can be spelled _____, _____, or _____.

The /ow/ sound can be spelled _____ or _____.

The /oi/ sound can be spelled _____ or _____.

The /ŏŏ/ sound is spelled _____.

The /ĕ/ sound is spelled _____.

➡️ Identify the types of syllables that are listed below. Use this code:

VC   for closed syllables

VC*e*   for silent-*e* syllables

CV   for open syllables

V*r*   for *r*-controlled syllables

Mark the long and short vowels and read the syllables to another student.

nē	CV	de	_____	umph	_____
id	_____	dine	_____	li	_____
tri	_____	sis	_____	mu	_____
et	_____	min	_____	cli	_____
cre	_____	der	_____	cam	_____
vi	_____	um	_____	o	_____
neer	_____	fu	_____	os	_____

➡️ Your teacher will dictate ten syllables for you to spell. Repeat the syllables aloud while spelling.

1. _____ _____   6. _____ _____

2. _____ _____   7. _____ _____

3. _____ _____   8. _____ _____

4. _____ _____   9. _____ _____

5. _____ _____   10. _____ _____

➡️ Using the code, identify the types of syllables you just spelled.

RULE

The **V/V Syllabication Rule (V/V):** If two vowels together do not make a recognizable word when sounded as a double vowel, divide between the vowels. This gives the first of the two vowels its long sound.

➤ Mark the vowels short (˘), long (¯), or schwa (ə), and combine the syllables to read the whole word. Then circle the syllables as shown.

trī	əl	(trial)
re	act	react
cre	ate	create
ru	in	ruin
cha	os	chaos
po	et	poet
qui	et	quiet

tri	umph		triumph
co	erce		coerce
sci	ence		science
i	de	a	idea
I	o	wa	Iowa
in	flu	ence	influence
mu	se	um	museum

➤ Unscramble the syllables to make a recognizable word.

cle	nu	us	_____
o	de	ro	_____
lin	vi	o	_____
pi	neer	o	_____
dine	i	o	_____
sis	a	o	_____
u	et	min	_____
an	me	der	_____
ence	in	flu	_____
o	vi	lence	_____

➤ The last syllable in the following words has the schwa sound. In this position, it is always spelled with the letter *a*. Add the *a* and copy the whole word. Then make up a sentence using two of the words.

*i de _____   _____   i o t _____   _____

l o w _____   _____   bo _____   _____

_____

_____

➤ *et* is a common spelling for the /ət/ or /it/ sound at the end of words. Fill in the blanks with *et*, copy the whole word, and then arrange the words in alphabetical order.

Add *et*	Copy	ABC Order
*po _____	_____	_____
*qui _____	_____	_____
viol _____	_____	_____
*di _____	_____	_____
su _____	_____	_____

➤ *ent* and *ant* are common spelling patterns for the schwa sound /ənt/ at the end of words. Add the final syllables as shown and copy the words.

Add *ent*		Add *ant*	
cli _____	_____	tru _____	_____
flu _____	_____	de fi _____	_____
*vi o l_____	_____		

➤ Have another student test you on spelling the starred words. They are practical spelling words.

My score: _____ words correct.

➡ Your teacher will dictate twelve words. Repeat the word, isolate the missing syllable, and spell it. Then write the whole word, saying it aloud as you spell.

1. _____ on   _____

2. _____ id   _____

3. po _____   _____

4. _____ o lin   _____

5. cre _____   _____

6. i _____ a   _____

7. l o _____   _____

8. _____ se _____   _____

9. ro _____ o   _____

10. i o _____   _____

11. _____ et   _____

12. in _____ ence   _____

➡ Choose three of the words above and write them in sentences.

_____

_____

_____

_____

_____

_____

★ The **V/V Syllabication Rule** is the last and least common syllabication rule. Only a few words divide between the vowels. The vowel in the first syllable is always long since the syllable is open. In most, but not all, cases the accent is on the first syllable.

➡ Divide between the vowels and mark the first vowel of the V/V combination long. Write the word by syllables and note the accent pattern.

Two-Syllable Words   **Three- and Four-Syllable Words**

nḗon | ne | _on_   meteor | me | _te_   _or_

lion | | _____   oasis   _____ | | _____

duet   _____ | | violin   _____   _____ | |

poet | | _____   Iowa | | _____   _____

create   _____ | | museum   _____ | | _____

diet | | _____   nucleus | | _____   _____

truant | | _____   chaotic   _____ | | _____

quiet | | _____   influence | | _____   _____

boa | | _____   continuum   _____ | | _____   _____

➡ Some of the words listed here are one-syllable words that contain a double vowel (VV). Other words are two-syllable words that divide between the vowels (V/V). Sound out the words and decide if they are one-syllable or two-syllable words. Then write them under the correct heading.

suit	lion	science	boa
quiet	spoil	pie	poach
trial	react	toe	dial
paint	preach	poet	jail
truant	ruin	fruit	duet

One-Syllable Words (VV)

_____

_____

_____

_____

_____

_____

_____

_____

_____

Two-Syllable Words (V/V)

_____

_____

_____

_____

_____

_____

_____

_____

_____

_____

_____

Proofing Practice

➡ Two common List 8 words are misspelled in each of the sentences below. Correct them as shown.

1. It seemed ~~crule~~ *cruel* of the lyon to kill the ostrich.

2. My client's triel began in a quite courtroom and ended in a chaotic one.

3. Diana had a novel ideah fro a sience fair project.

4. The pome was about a dule between Romeo and his rival.

➡ The /əl/ sound at the end of some common V/V words is spelled with *al* or *el*. Circle the last two letters in each of the following words. Then write them under the correct heading.

trial	duel	ideal	real
cruel	dial	fuel	

al   *el*

_____   _____

_____   _____

_____   _____

_____

➡ The /ən/ sound in these common words is spelled with *on*. Fill in the blanks with *on* and write the whole word.

li __ __   _____   pi __ __ eer   _____

➡ Complete the puzzle with the words from above.

Across

2. a perfect type
5. the process of trying or testing; trying a case in court
7. not fake

Down

1. You have to _____ when you use the phone.
3. a fight between two people to settle a quarrel
4. mean; causing pain
6. Gas is a kind of _____.

➡ Have another student test you on spelling these common words.

My score: _____ words correct.

➡ Match the definitions to the words. Use your dictionary.

neon	1. easy flowing; good in language	_____
truant	2. very small amount	_____
triumph	3. openly resisting	_____
nucleus	4. gas used in signs	_____
cameo	5. child who skips school	_____
fluent	6. central part of an atom	_____
defiant	7. stone used for jewelry	_____
iota	8. victory; success	_____

➡ The words at the bottom of the page are words you are likely to use in spelling. Be sure to learn how to spell them. Fill in the blanks with words that make sense in the sentences.

1. A good _____ includes lots of fruits and vegetables.

2. Mr. Leopold is on _____ for murder.

3. The _____ on the radio doesn't work.

4. The famous _____ wrote a short _____ about springtime.

5. The _____ in the cage roared; it was not a _____ sound.

6. Do you have any _____ what time it is? I have a feeling it's

_____ late.

7. Violet and Joel worked in the lab in _____ class today.

8. The two _____ men fought a _____ .

poet	science	really	dial
quiet	lion	diet	idea
trial	duel	poem	cruel

➡ Read the following sentences and circle all the List 8 words that you can find.

1. The idea inspired the poet to create a poem.

2. Which animal would you fear more, a lion or a boa constrictor?

3. The defiant pioneer braved the cruel, Iowa winter.

4. The model of a nucleus at the science museum is novel.

5. The violin duet was followed by a lively minuet.

6. Staying on his diet was a major triumph for Romeo.

7. The neon light made everything look violet.

8. Andrea is a quiet student who would never riot.

9. Dial this number if you want a good deal on fuel.

10. Salt can provide the iodine needed in our diet.

11. If you try to coerce the truant to go back to school, he might react with violence.

➡ Take out a piece of blank paper. Your teacher will dictate three of the sentences above for you to write.

➡ Now select ten words from List 8 and create a short story or a descriptive paragraph that uses those words. Be creative and avoid repetition!

Reading Accuracy: Demonstrate your accuracy in reading and spelling List 8 words. Your teacher will select ten words to read and ten practical spelling words for you to spell. Record your scores on the Accuracy Checklist. Work toward 90–100 percent accuracy.

Reading Proficiency: Now build up your reading fluency with List 8 words. Decide on your rate goal with your teacher. Record your progress on the Proficiency Graph.

My goal for reading List 8 is _____ words per minute with two or fewer errors.

* anything	* kitten	* ribbon	drugstore	publish
* bacon	* legal	* rival	eagle	punish
* basic	* lemon	* rubber	escort	puppet
* basket	* limit	* salad	explode	rodeo
* carbon	* lion	* sermon	further	ruin
* collide	* locate	* study	humid	sailboat
* complete	* menu	* subject	hustle	sherbet
* copy	* model	* sunshine	insane	silver
* costume	* necktie	* without	intrude	snowball
* crater	* oatmeal	absorb	invade	sober
* cruel	* partner	athlete	Iowa	suppose
* everyone	* poet	bugle	lobster	surplus
* handle	* prison	camel	mental	temple
* happen	* problem	chaos	noble	tiny
* idea	* purple	curtsy	oasis	tonsil
* item	* puzzle	daytime	outlaw	twinkle
* kettle	* quiet	dictate	pretzel	unit

*Practical spelling words. The teacher and student should decide together how many of these words the student will be responsible for spelling.

Closed (VC)	A closed syllable has only one vowel and ends in a consonant. The vowel is usually short: *ad, sug, lish, trom, ject.*
Silent-*e* (VC*e*)	A silent-*e* syllable has one vowel followed by a consonant followed by an *e*. The *e* is silent and makes the preceding vowel long: *plete, mune, stroke, ope, mate.*
Open (CV)	An open syllable ends in one vowel. The vowel is usually long: *pi, glo, stri, u, cy, re.*
***r*-Controlled (V*r*)**	An *r*-controlled syllable has a vowel followed by an *r*, which modifies the vowel sound: *car, mer, fir, cor, tur.*
Consonant-*le* (C*le*)	A consonant-*le* syllable is a final syllable in which the *e* is silent; thus it sounds like a consonant-əl: *ta-ble, jungle, sim-ple, bu-gle.*
Double-Vowel (VV)	A double-vowel syllable has two vowels that together make one sound. This sound has to be learned, as it often takes on a sound different from either single vowel: *boat, fie, haul, voy, floun.*

VC/CV	When two or more consonants stand between two vowels, divide between the consonants, keeping blends or digraphs together: *pup-pet, hun-<u>dred</u>, sup-pose, fan-tas-tic.*
V/CV	When a single consonant is surrounded by two vowels, the most common division is before the consonant, making the vowel in the first syllable long: *hu-man, lo-cate, pi-lot, e-ven.*
VC/V	If the V/CV Syllabication Rule doesn't make a recognizable word, divide after the consonant and give the vowel its short sound: *rap-id, sol-id, cab-in, stud-y.*
/C*le*	Divide before the consonant-*le*. Count back three letters from the end of the word and divide: *star-tle, sta-ble, am-ble, ea-gle.*
V/V	Only a few words divide between the vowels: *di-et, flu-id, qui-et, i-o-dine.*

Student _____

Record accuracy score as a fraction: $\dfrac{\text{# correct}}{\text{# attempted}}$

List	Examples	Check Test Scores Date:		Reading			Spelling		
		Reading	**Spelling**						
1. Compound Words	without haystack								
2. VC/CV Closed Syllables	tonsil splendid								
3. VC/CV Closed and Silent-*e* Syllables	stampede escape								
4. VC/CV Closed and *r*-Controlled Syllables	lobster garlic								
5. V/CV	tulip raven								
6. VC/V	relish comet								
7. /C*le*	stumble purple								
8. V/V	diet fluid								
Review: Lists 1–8									

PROFICIENCY GRAPH

Student _____

Goal _____

●———● Words Read Correctly

x———x Errors

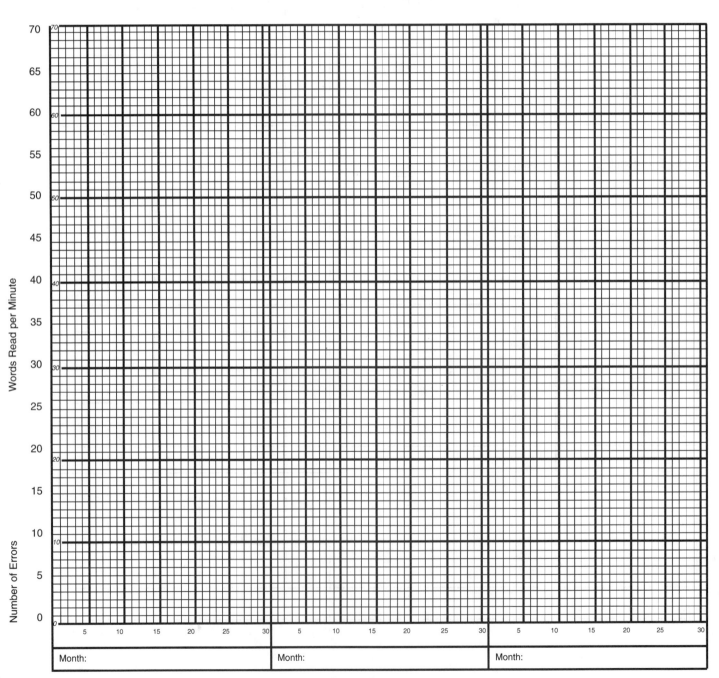

Words Read per Minute

Number of Errors

Month: _____   Month: _____   Month: _____

Calendar Days

PROFICIENCY GRAPH

Student _____

Goal _____

●———● Words Read Correctly

✗———✗ Errors

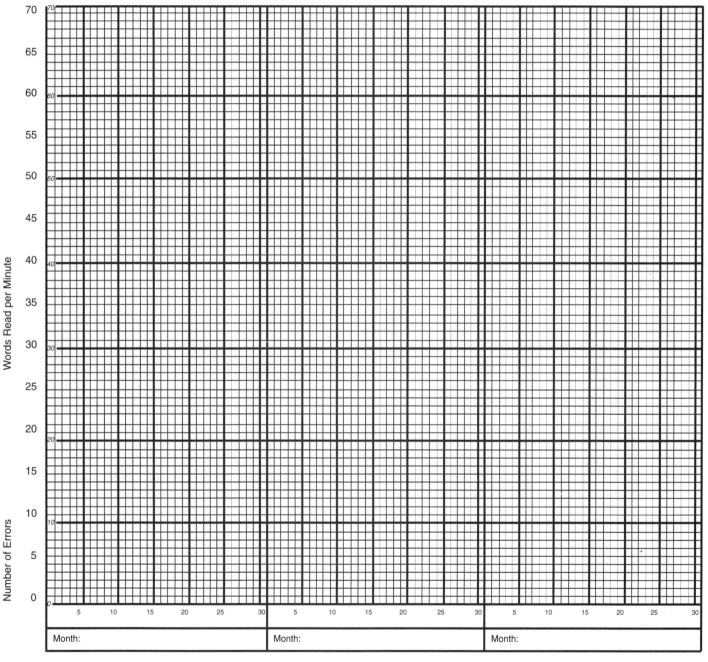

Words Read per Minute

Number of Errors

Calendar Days

Month:

Month:

Month:

Student _____

Goal _____

●————● Words Read Correctly

✕————✕ Errors

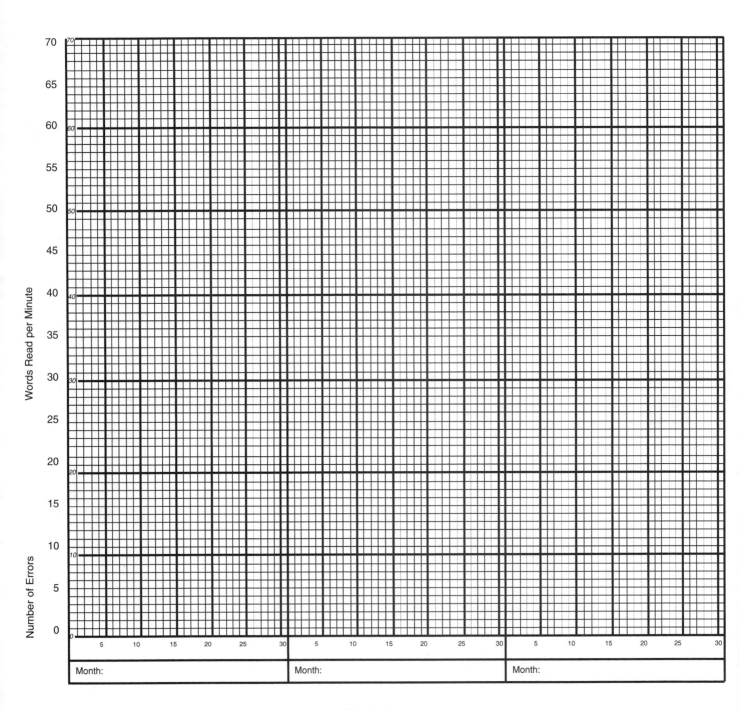

Words Read per Minute

Number of Errors

| | Month: | Month: | Month: |

Calendar Days

EXAMINER'S RECORDING FORM – READING

Check Test: Lists 1-8

Megawords 1

Name _____   Date _____

1. Compound Words

handball
mailbox
anywhere
barefoot
playmate

correct _____

2. VC/CV Closed Syllables

splendid
basket
coffin
establish
fantastic

correct _____

3. VC/CV Closed and Silent-e Syllables

trombone
commune
reptile
indispose
confiscate

correct _____

4. VC/CV Closed and r-Controlled Syllables

hermit
morbid
urban
permanent
carpenter

correct _____

5. V/CV

virus
veto
cupid
pilot
basin

correct _____

6. VC/V

rapid
denim
topic
punish
comic

correct _____

7. /Cle

cable
tremble
hustle
startle
ankle

correct _____

8. V/V

boa
fluid
diet
meander
iodine

correct _____

Total Correct _____
Total Possible __40__

Name _____   Date _____

1. Compound Words

handball
mailbox
anywhere
barefoot
playmate

correct _____

2. VC/CV Closed Syllables

splendid
basket
coffin
establish
fantastic

correct _____

3. VC/CV Closed and Silent-e Syllables

trombone
commune
reptile
indispose
confiscate

correct _____

4. VC/CV Closed and r–Controlled Syllables

hermit
morbid
urban
permanent
carpenter

correct _____

5. V/CV

virus
veto
cupid
pilot
basin

correct _____

6. VC/V

rapid
denim
topic
punish
comic

correct _____

7. /Cle

cable
tremble
hustle
startle
ankle

correct _____

8. V/V

boa
fluid
diet
meander
iodine

correct _____

Total Correct _____
Total Possible ___40___